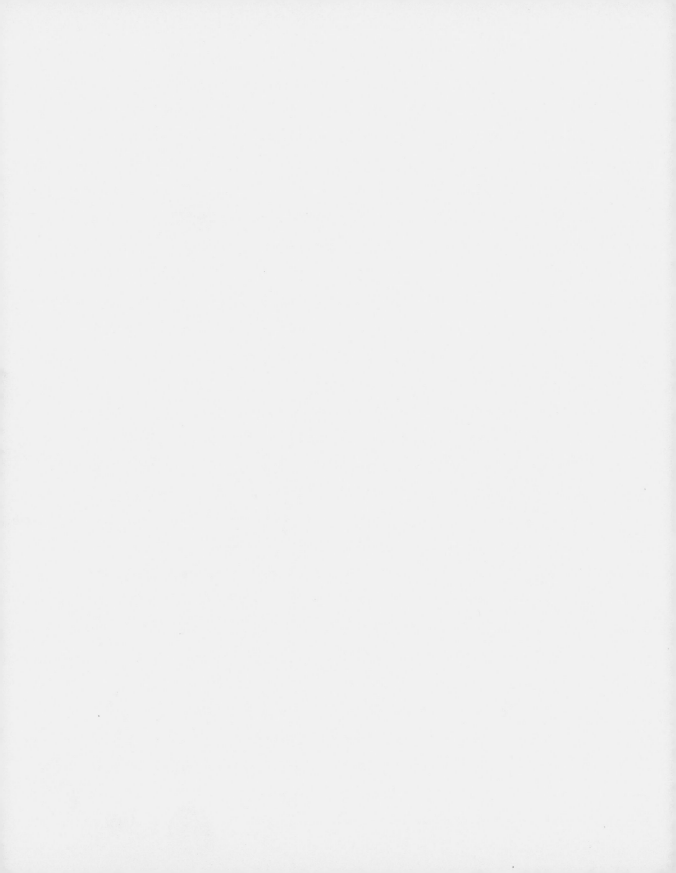

smoothie project

The *28-Day Plan* to Feel Happy and Healthy No Matter Your Age

Catherine McCord

Photography by Colin Price

Abrams, New York

Contents

Introduction:
You Can Change Your Life in 28 Days

This is the smoothie book for everyone. Most smoothie books focus solely on dieting, detoxing, and cleansing (which, don't get me wrong, are important subjects, and I will cover them in the pages that follow), but I've discovered that when it comes to the wellness and therapeutic potential of smoothies, these are merely the tip of the proverbial iceberg. Smoothies can be used to effectively address an incredibly wide range of health and nutritional issues—weight loss, eating right, pregnancy, nursing, feeding kids of all ages, from babies to teens—as well as many chronic health conditions such as anxiety, ADHD, depression, eczema, nausea, stress, and promoting weight gain during cancer treatment. Smoothies have a great deal more to offer—for anyone, at any stage of life— and my mission in writing this book is to show you how they can change your life for the better.

This book also demonstrates just how easy, fun, and delicious incorporating smoothies into your daily routine can be. My advice is based on an approach to food that I developed in the decade-plus of running my family food business, Weelicious, where I devise strategies to make cooking a simple, healthful, and affordable

experience for families. So when I discovered the healing properties of smoothies, I applied that same Weelicious philosophy to making them. Because one smoothie a day really can make a difference in your quality of life, and who doesn't want an easy way to do that?

We have become all too accustomed to strict and complicated diet plans we're told can improve our health, so I understand how the simple idea that smoothies can be life-changing might seem a bit absurd at first.

But I have been on the Smoothie Project journey since 2015, and I have witnessed the impact it has had on members of the online #smoothieproject community who have gone on this odyssey with me. I've been moved by the powerful accounts of people who have overcome a wide spectrum of health challenges and accomplished major lifestyle goals with the help of smoothies. I have observed firsthand how transformative smoothies can be for families (my own included)—for every single member, no matter what their age, health, goals, likes, and dislikes are.

However, addressing each person's particular needs requires some careful curating. When you

take into account lifestyle goals, health issues, or even individual flavor preferences, each of us will want and need different things from a smoothie; especially when it comes to health benefits, weeding through the overwhelming amount of nutritional information out there in order to decipher what our bodies can benefit most from can leave us feeling confused and hopeless. So with this book I set out to address individual concerns and guide every age group, from babies to baby boomers and everyone in between.

Think of this book as your Smoothie Bible— a comprehensive, only-one-you'll-ever-need collection of the best smoothie recipes with detailed advice on everything from nutrition to convenience. It will inspire you throughout the year and grow with you, accommodating both your changing needs and tastes.

You'll see how you can rid your diet of foods that may be making your body fight back and turn on you, and also how easy it is to replace them with foods that will optimize your physical, mental, and emotional states of being.

No matter your age, lifestyle goals, or the current quality of your health, in this busy, faster, seemingly always-connected 24/7 world, the basic foundations of self-care—sleeping, exercise, and eating well—are harder than ever to maintain. That's why I am challenging you (and your family) to take just a few minutes each morning for twenty-eight days to start your day with a smoothie using the recipes in the pages that follow. It's that simple.

"Where," you may be wondering, "did this twenty-eight-day number come from?"—a good question to ask given that I have been on the daily smoothie plan for almost five years. The answer is twofold: First, twenty-eight days is more or less the time it took for a smoothie regimen to turn around the health issues troubling my own family. Second, years of research and hearing from others using smoothies therapeutically confirmed that significant results could be achieved in that amount of time.

If you make the commitment to adding a nutrient-dense smoothie to your daily diet for just twenty-eight days, this book can be a force of positive change in your life. And, if the benefits experienced by my family, as well as the scores of Weelicious followers who went on this years-long journey with me have proven anything, you'll be excited to keep going.

No matter your reason for picking up this book, the easy-to-adopt lifestyle shift of drinking smoothies will get you started on a path to feeling and looking your very best.

Catherine

This is the smoothie book for everyone

The Origin of the Smoothie Project

My evangelical embrace of smoothies began with a challenging health situation with my son (my son is also the person who unintentionally inspired Weelicious, the family food company I founded in 2007, so we like to say that he is my muse).

In January 2015, when my son was eight, he started complaining of constant nausea, headaches, stomachaches, and general fatigue. It was a daily refrain that began each morning when he woke up and continued throughout the day, right up until the moment he went to bed; it persisted for months. After several visits to the doctor's office and a battery of tests, our pediatrician told us he could find nothing discernibly wrong. While that certainly was a relief, watching my little boy continue to cope with these unpleasant symptoms every day was breaking my heart.

My Journey Begins

Needing to start somewhere, I turned to an area I have a lot of experience with: nutrition. I adore the doctors who treat our family; however, I've never found comprehensive nutritional advice to be a strong suit of Western medicine. Between nutrition not being taught in depth in medical school and Big Pharma spending a fortune to convince us all (doctors included) that there is a pill to cure everything, most of the doctors I know cannot even begin to address the things that ail us through what we eat. Beyond offering preventative advice, such as avoiding foods high in sugar and saturated fat, most doctors never even consider food as a remedy. That's kind of ironic when the age-old adage is "an apple a day keeps the doctor away," but there's twenty-first-century Western medicine for you.

I had always believed that my son's diet was reasonably healthy for a kid his age (obviously with a lot of help, guidance, and occasional arm twisting from his parents). A vegetarian since the age of six (a decision he made completely on his own), my son has always had a love for a wide variety of fruits and vegetables. He more or less eats almost completely organic, consumes little to no processed food, and completely avoids food dyes, so eliminating things like nitrates and synthetic chemicals as potential culprits was easy for me to do. That still left a lot of nutrition to explore, so I began reading countless books and talking to nutritionists, allergists, and other specialists about what could be at the root of my son's issues. Over time, his breakfasts had become pretty carb heavy. He was almost always requesting pancakes, waffles, crepes, toast and butter, and French toast, and, like many parents, I fell into the trap of indulging him, believing that the rest of his diet was good and that since I was making almost all of those things homemade, with good organic ingredients, it wasn't causing any real harm.

Finding a Needle in a Haystack

In the midst of my seemingly endless research, I came across an interview with a fascinating clinical nutritionist named Kelly Dorfman, who "is one of the world's foremost experts in using nutrition therapeutically to improve brain function, energy, and mood."[1] In 2013, she wrote *Cure Your Child with Food*, which explores the hidden connections between food and childhood ailments such as anxiety, recurrent ear infections, stomachaches, ADHD, and more. This was a big moment for me: Dorfman was approaching treatment of chronic, elusive conditions with food and having significant results. I felt like I had been rummaging through a huge informational haystack up until that point, and suddenly, I happened upon the needle. It opened my eyes to the likelihood that those foods my son was starting each morning with—the waffles, pancakes, and other foods rich in wheat and dairy—were having a negative impact on his health and how he felt on a daily basis. Now I had to prove it.

For some reason, while I was reading *Cure Your Child with Food*, a word caught my attention: *smoothies*. Dorfman puts no particular emphasis on smoothies nor does she offer guidelines for how to employ them therapeutically. However, for someone who spends most of her waking moments thinking about the simplest and most enjoyable ways to get good nutrition into kids, the ease of that suggestion struck a chord with me. A daily smoothie regimen seemed like a great (and hopefully fun) way to expose to my son to a variety of different nutrient-dense foods without him feeling like a drastic dietary change was being imposed on him, and it also would enable me to test what impact, if any, diet was having on my son's symptoms.

This investigation would take a few weeks to produce results—not to mention it would require the cooperation of a kid who was very attached to his well-established daily breakfast routine. And just as I feared, when I told my son what we were going to do—even though I emphasized that this change was potentially going to make him feel better—he was not at all receptive of my grand plan to eliminate pancakes in favor of making smoothies the new cornerstone of his diet. His answer was an unambiguous "no." So I got creative.

The Experiment

Affording kids a degree of control over their meals is essential, and I knew that this situation with my son would be no exception. Making him an active participant in this experiment would make all the difference in whether it succeeded or not. I informed my son that contrary to what he might be thinking, that *he*—not I—was going to be in charge of how we did this; *he* would be the one choosing what went in his smoothie every day. You might suspect this idea would be a disaster in the making—chocolate chip pancake smoothies, anyone? However, while I was absolutely committed to the idea of giving my son autonomy over his morning meal, I had a master plan for how to quietly guide the whole process. Each night before bed, I gave my son an informal menu of nutritious fruits, vegetables, and add-ins and asked him to circle the items he wanted me to put in his smoothie the next morning. Because the choice was all his, he bought in to this program. And since the ingredients he could choose from were determined by me, I had no fear of requests for chocolate chips, cookie dough, or any other crazy item in his smoothies. And because I made sure to always present him with a lot of options, he never felt like he was being put in a box.

Feeling empowered by this process, my son didn't just enjoy our new morning mealtime system, he actually looked forward to it, and over the next few weeks, I successfully eliminated all of the morning eggs, bread, cheese, and refined sugar. The best part? In less than one month, everything that had been ailing my son disappeared. Completely.

1. www.kellydorfman.com/about-kelly-dorfman

An Unanticipated Response

I neglected to mention that during the time I was treating my son with smoothies, I still had two other hungry little mouths to feed every morning: my two daughters (who at the time were seven years and ten months old, respectively). Readers of my first cookbook may recall that the subtitle is "One Family. One Meal." This expression stems from my strongly held belief that no parent should be a short-order cook, making each family member something different to eat at mealtime. This meant that since my son was getting smoothies for breakfast every day, my daughters were getting them, too.

As any parent knows, babies require constant supervision, making completing even the simplest of tasks a challenge. So, in order to keep my ten-month-old entertained in the morning—as well as to introduce her to new foods and cooking—I'd sit her next to the blender, have her help me fill it with the smoothie ingredients, and let her press the power button. When the smoothie was poured, she (in what was clearly an early display of pride of ownership) would immediately lean over and start sipping (it's worth noting that more than three years later, the first thing she asks for every morning still is her smoothie). I found this so adorable that I started posting daily videos of it on Instagram.

However, what for me just seemed like sharing some cute moments of my baby's insatiable appetite for smoothies was being received by a large number of people as a sort of call to action—and within a few weeks, I noticed that something incredible was happening. With each passing day, I was receiving more and more reactions, questions, and personal stories from people who were clearly taken with this baby's love of smoothies. These videos, along with the story of my son's health success drinking them, had become a kind of daily inspiration for them, and in turn they felt compelled to share with me the impact that smoothies were having on them and their families. Whether a person's goal was to feel better while pregnant, introduce a baby or toddler to new food, help to cure an ailing loved one, or simply change what they put into their body at the beginning of every day, smoothies were making an enormous difference in a lot of people's lives, and I was watching—almost in real time—the variety of ways people were utilizing smoothies to change their health.

I felt like I was witnessing the birth of a movement, and it compelled me to unify this community. I actively encouraged people to share their smoothie success stories, in hopes of motivating and influencing others looking for help, and bringing greater awareness to the various health issues people were overcoming with smoothies.

I felt like I was witnessing the birth of a movement

#SMOOTHIEPROJECT

From that point forward I posted all my smoothie content under the hashtag #smoothieproject. Almost immediately, people began partaking in the conversation, posting pictures and videos of their smoothies and sharing their challenges and triumphs with an ever-growing #smoothieproject community. I was so moved by the intimacy of these stories that I couldn't wait to post a new story of my own each day just to see where the conversation would go.

Over the course of this experience, I became enlightened. The potential health benefits of smoothies were more far-reaching than I had ever imagined, impacting people from a wide range of age groups and with diverse health struggles. The stories I have received over the years cover so many types of ailments and challenges, it inspired me to dedicate a section of this book to some of them and the ways to address them with smoothies (see pages 233 to 236).

How to Use This Book

The hardest part about writing a book on nutrition is that we're all built differently. What works for or is appealing to one person may not hold true for another. That's why I consulted with specialists and nutritional experts, so I could recommend smoothies to accommodate a wide variety of needs and palates.

Getting the Most out of This Book

The goal of this book is to help you change your health and the way you feel within twenty-eight days of implementing it, so the more specific you can be with your improvement goals, the more you will get out of it. Then the fun part begins: discovering what kinds of smoothies are right for you.

Every time I make a smoothie for me or my family, I view it as a new opportunity. I consider what may be going on in our bodies, and that determines what I add to the blender. Is one of us coming down with a cold or lacking energy? Have my husband or I been eating recklessly lately and need some nutritional discipline? Or do I simply feel like my engine is not running as efficiently as it should?

Take a moment to really think about what you want to accomplish. What is your body telling you? How exactly do you want to change the way you're feeling? Some of you may have something very specific you want to change, while others may have more general concerns.

The **Getting the Most Out of Your Ingredients** chapter (pages 238 to 241) highlights ingredients (and particular smoothie recipes) that are ideal for certain age groups and for addressing particular issues or achieving your unique goals. This chapter also features a chart that is intended to demystify what most people find to be a bewildering array of supplements, powders, oils, and other add-ins that you can use to amplify the nutritional impact of your smoothie. The chart will help you identify ingredients that you can use to customize your smoothies to your specific needs.

The **Tools of the Trade** chapter (pages 36 to 39) features a comprehensive list of what you need to make great smoothies (spoiler alert: not much!). In it, I highlight some of my personal favorite smoothie products and why I love them so much.

Throughout the book, you'll also see smoothie hacks, tips, and tricks for making a smoothie lifestyle as convenient as possible.

Medical and Nutritional Advice

While I consider myself well-versed in many of the health benefits of a smoothie regimen, I'm neither a doctor nor a nutritional professional. For that reason, I relied on a respected collection of experts like Kelly Dorfman, MS, LDN; Keri Glassman, MS, RD, CDN; Ashley Koff, RD; and Whitney English Tabaie, MS, RDN to support the results and provide the science behind the recommendations made in this book. It's worth adding that all of these experts also are accomplished authors in their own right, and their writing has both educated and inspired me in my journey. And, of course, it goes without saying that you should always speak to your physician about any health concerns that you may have.

The Recipes

The recipes in this book are organized in chapters primarily by flavor profile, so if you are in the mood for something specific, it should be easy to figure out where to turn. Most chapter titles are straightforward, but a couple benefit from some explanation:

Clean + Clear features smoothies like Detox (page 137) and Light and Bright (page 138) that are more fruit and vegetable based, and use water, herbal tea, or coconut water in lieu of milk.

The ingredients in **Healing + Supporting** focus primarily on the health and wellness issues identified in the recipe titles, like Immunity Booster (page 173) and Skin Brightener (page 186).

Green helps you focus on deliciously getting in those all-important greens without the bitter taste some people associate with kale, spinach, and other verdant veggies.

Vanilla + Chocolate + Coffee + Matcha contains smoothies that feature these unique flavors. I grouped these four ingredients together, as they have singular, distinct flavor profiles and tend to cohabitate in the food world. The coffee and matcha recipes are also perfect if you're looking for a healthy smoothie that does the double duty of delivering a caffeine boost (by the way, it's easy to add a little coffee or matcha to many of the recipes in this book; see page 20 for tips on how to do so).

Each of the recipes serves one person and will create a 10-ounce to 14-ounce drink. The variation in volume is due to the slightly different sizes of fresh produce and the varying amounts of water they can provide.

Time challenged during the week? Make a big batch of smoothies on Sunday; divide it among seven mason jars, filling them three-quarters full, seal the jars tightly, and then freeze. Transfer a jar to the fridge to defrost each night, then in the morning simply give it a shake and you're ready to go. For more on freezing and making smoothies in advance, see pages 30 to 33.

The Magical World of Super Boosts

Each recipe also includes a list of optional super boosts, supplements you can add to your smoothie to amplify its nutritional impact (I recommend following the serving suggestion listed on the packaging). Don't get overwhelmed by these. Remember, you don't need to add any super boosts (the recipes are designed to be healthy without them). But super boosts offer an easy way to take your smoothie-making game up a nutritional level. While you can add as few or as many as you like, ideally pick two or three that you feel you would benefit from. The super boosts listed for each smoothie suit its flavor profile and texture while promoting nutrient absorption (see pages 238 to 241 for a detailed breakdown of super boosts). But remember, they are simply suggestions—feel free to be creative and try other ingredients that suit your particular nutritional needs. You can't go wrong.

Why Smoothies?

Oh, how I love answering this question. From nutrition, to convenience, to affordability, to fun (healthy ice cream, what?!), smoothies can make your life better in so many ways. They are just about as practical as food gets. You'll see for yourself how true all that is, but in case you need a bit of convincing, keep reading. . . .

Great for Your Health . . . and a Whole Lot More

Here are seven key reasons to give smoothies a try:

1. **They save (a lot of) time:** You'd be hard-pressed to find a healthier, more well-rounded way of eating that takes less time to prepare. They're a complete meal that can be made in a matter of minutes—it's as easy as dump, blend, and pour. They're even faster than grabbing prepared food from the supermarket.

2. **They're portable:** You can take them anywhere. All you need is a container or glass with an airtight lid that fits in your car's cup holder and you can enjoy a healthy meal anywhere.

3. **They're economical:** Making smoothies doesn't require expensive kitchen tools or equipment. Plus, if you're using your blender every day, it pays for itself. A decent one can be found online for around $20 and a very good one can be found for $50. See page 38 for my top picks, and see page 18 to learn just how cost-effective smoothies can be.

4. **They prevent waste:** Smoothies allow you to clean out your fridge by either using the food you have on hand or freezing your surplus ripe fruit and vegetables and using them in a smoothie at a later date. See page 33 for easy freezing tips.

5. **They're a way of eating that the realities of life can't sabotage:** When you travel, how often do you find your usual way of eating challenged by a lack of available healthy choices? By simply arming yourself with an inexpensive travel blender and locating the closest supermarket at your destination, you're all set. These days, fresh organic fruits and vegetables are widely available. And if the local market features a less-than-desirable fresh produce selection, high-quality frozen fruit and vegetables are pretty easy to come by.

6. **They're monotony-proof:** The flavor combinations are endless, so you likely won't tire of smoothies. You can alter the taste, ingredients, consistency, and flavor depending on your cravings, seasonality, and/or what happens to be available in your kitchen. Not in the mood to drink your morning meal? Go heavier on the frozen fruit and veggies and turn your smoothie into a bowl. It's equally healthy and delicious, and it fills you up—what I refer to as the mealtime trifecta.

7. **They help you start your day the right way:** Even with the best of intentions, life can get in the way of exercise or throw poor eating options in our path. By starting with a nutrient-packed, easy-to-digest smoothie in the morning, you are setting a positive, healthy tone for your day. You can be confident that your body is getting so much of what it needs right off the bat.

Smoothies Are Fun

Dieting sucks. Too often healthy eating is devoid of pleasure—yet another necessity to tick off of our never-ending to-do lists. Food should be fun, but in our busy lives, where meals often are squeezed in rather than savored, the routine-ification of eating right can be the norm. And eating the same thing every day is boring.

Aside from a desire to eat healthfully, one reason people go to smoothie shops is because they make the options fun. Getting to choose a flavor combo based on how you feel in the moment is kind of exciting, and changing it up keeps things fresh.

It's easy to replicate that experience at home.

An effective smoothie regimen does not mean having to pick one recipe and stick with it for a long period of time. You can enjoy something different every day, and therein lies the fun: the variety of flavors, textures, and nutrients you get to choose from. Try seeking out ingredients that may be unfamiliar but that seem interesting to you. Look at the Smoothie Project as a way to mix things up and get healthy in a pleasurable way.

While I have my favorite smoothie recipes that I make for myself time and again, since starting #smoothieproject almost five years ago, I'm not exaggerating when I say that I've made my kids a different flavor combination almost every day of the year. My kids still look forward to coming into the kitchen in the morning to see what that day's concoction is going to be. And by varying the ingredients, I'm ensuring that our bodies are consistently getting a vast assortment of essential vitamins and nutrients.

Smoothies Are Affordable

"That smoothie looks expensive. How much does it cost?" That's a comment I often see in my Instagram feed.

My knee-jerk reaction is "Expensive when compared to what?" Meaning what would you be eating instead, and how does it stack up in a cost-versus-benefit analysis. Are there cheaper ways to eat than making a smoothie? Of course, although I'd argue that many of those options are not advisable if health and good nutrition are of primary importance to you. Quality produce and assorted supplements are certainly not cheap, but smoothies are still the most cost-effective vehicle for consuming a wide variety of the most essential foods we should be eating in one meal.

Looking at the big picture is important. In isolation, supplements and organic produce can seem costly; however, a bag of chia seeds or frozen mango will last you a long time, making the cost per smoothie a pretty competitive option. When you're maintaining a daily smoothie regimen, there is little to no waste of food or money—you're using your ingredients. Still, many smoothie ingredients either have long shelf lives or are (or can be) frozen, so even if you're not making smoothies every day, your ingredient supply isn't going to quickly spoil and waste your investment.

How Affordable Are They?

The following smoothie comparisons are all based on organic ingredients priced out on Instacart for Whole Foods in Los Angeles. Your numbers will of course vary depending on the costs where you live and what brands you select, but it should offer you a good general idea:

AVERAGE DAILY COST OF MAKING YOUR OWN SMOOTHIES

Mango Spice (page 41) $2.95

Sweet Green (page 75) $2.70

Matcha Date Shake (page 100) $1.75

Blue Chia (page 113) $2.05

Average Daily Cost **$2.36**

SMOOTHIES FOR	COST OF MAKING	COST OF BUYING*
7 Days	$16.53	$70.67
28 Days	$66.08	$282.66
1 Year	$861.40	$3,684.68

Average cost of Kreation's Enlighten Smoothie and Le Pain Quotidien's Super Greens Smoothie multiplied by number of days.

Here's yet another way to look at it: the cost of your food vs. the cost of health care. There are many sobering statistics about the American diet and its relationship to the skyrocketing cost of medical care. While I won't bore you with facts and figures here, it's unnerving to see just how many of the medical conditions plaguing our population are rooted in diet. Healthy eating certainly doesn't guarantee one won't have medical issues in the future, but there's an overwhelming amount of research supporting the long-term health benefits of a diet rich in organic produce. And if you contract a chronic nutrition- and obesity-related ailment, such as heart disease, the associated medical bills will likely significantly eclipse the cost of consuming good food over the years. In addition, you're saving time—and, as they say, time is money.

SMOOTHIE HACK

Looking to save money? Don't overlook leftovers.
A handful of plain steamed vegetables from last
night's dinner, fruit salad, oatmeal, brown rice,
quinoa, kamut, even beans will boost the nutrition
(and lower the cost) of your smoothie.

Dependent on the caffeine jolt of your morning coffee? Smoothies with cold brew shots are a thing now. If you don't have cold brew on hand, make a pot of strong coffee, let it cool, pour the coffee into a silicone ice cube tray, and freeze, then just pop a few cubes into your favorite smoothie for a boost of caffeine. Coffee is a nice flavor complement to many of the recipes in this book, especially the earthier-tasting smoothies that are more vanilla, chocolate, seed, or nut forward. Matcha, another ingredient that has joined the "it" club, is another way to attain your caffeine boost. You can brew a pot of matcha tea and freeze it into cubes in the same way suggested above for coffee and use them in your smoothies. Its flavor generally won't be as pronounced as coffee (see pages 87 to 103 for smoothie recipes featuring coffee and matcha).

Smoothies Are Better Homemade

Restaurant meals tend to demand a certain level of culinary prowess or time to create, allowing us to rationalize the cost: I'll pay a premium for that chicken dish because I don't have the cooking skills to make it myself, and even if I did, it would take me too long to make it from scratch. That's not the case with smoothies. Even if you have no cooking skills you can produce smoothies of the highest quality in a fraction of the time it takes to buy them—my four-year-old can make one on her own. In spite of that, juice and smoothie joints like Kreation, Jamba Juice, and Qwench abound.

But when I think about how long it takes me to prepare a homemade smoothie in the morning versus driving and waiting in line for someone to make me the exact same thing, the decision to make it myself is a no-brainer—one made only more compelling by the significant amount of money I save doing it myself.

Below are two examples of store-bought smoothies I love (so much, in fact, that I re-created them for this book; see pages 72 and 138), comparing what they cost in-store versus what it costs me to make the same thing at home using organic ingredients:

Le Pain Quotidien's Super Greens Smoothie
Ingredients: *kale, celery, cucumber, lemon, pineapple, apple, ginger, mint, apple juice*

COST:
LPQ: $7.99
Homemade: $1.90
Savings: $6.09/smoothie

Kreation's Enlighten Me
Ingredients: *beet, lemon, apple, carrot, goji berry, coconut water, salt*

COST:
Kreation: $12.20
Homemade: $3.40
Savings: $8.80/smoothie

Sure, smoothie shops have their place, and when I'm out on the go I'm only too happy to have the option available to me. However, if you're someone who regularly frequents one of these places, it really makes you wonder what you're paying a premium for.

Smoothies Are Better Than Juice

These days you can find almost as many juice shops and smoothie shops as you can coffee bars. Deciding which option—smoothies or juice—is the better choice for you can be confusing.

I enjoy cold-pressed juices and frequent local places like Kreation, whose brand I believe is committed to the highest quality approach to juicing. However, I personally don't have the patience required for DIY juicing, as it can be quite messy, and the process leaves behind all the pulp of the fruit and vegetables. Juicers, many of which have removable parts, require considerably more cleaning than a blender does.

Juicing can also be an expensive proposition. First, consider that you are buying produce solely for its juice and discarding the rest (and it requires a disproportionate amount of produce to extract the desired amount of juice). Second, there's the equipment. Quality cold-press juicers (they do exactly what their name implies: they extract the juice from fruits and vegetables by pressing them through a strainer without producing heat in a process that preserves their delicate nutrients and enzymes) are preferable to the more common centrifugal variety. Those chop the fruits and vegetables and spin them at high speeds (a process that creates heat and in turn diminishes the produce's essential nutrients and enzymes) to obtain the juice. Centrifugal juicers are more affordable and relatively easier to clean than cold-press juicers, but there's a major nutritional sacrifice. Conversely, smoothie quality is far less dependent on the sophistication of the blender. While a high-end blender will produce a smoother smoothie, the nutritional value of a smoothie remains the same regardless of whether you paid $40 or $400 for your blender.

And even if ease and cost are not issues for you, fiber is an extremely important factor to consider.

Dietary Fiber

Fruits and vegetables are rich in essential vitamins and nutrients. They also contain dietary fiber, which slows digestion, regulating the absorption of nutrients in our bodies and helping to keep our digestive systems operating efficiently. Consuming fiber may also lower the risk of a number of serious illnesses.

While the role of fiber is certainly a lot more complicated than that, suffice it to say that it plays a very important role in our diets and is central to the juice vs. smoothie question.

SMOOTHIE HACK

Want (or need) to add more fiber to your diet? Add 2 to 3 tablespoons of rolled oats to your smoothie. If your blender is not particularly powerful, blend the oats before adding the other ingredients. Oats serve as both a fiber boost and a thickener.

Juicing vs. Blending

Juicing

When you juice fruits and vegetables, you are extracting much of the nutrients and liquid from the produce while getting rid of the fiber found in its flesh and skin. Removing the fiber makes it easier for our bodies to absorb the nutrients from the fruits and vegetables.

Quick absorption of nutrients is not a bad thing if you are solely juicing vegetables. It's a much different story, however, when it comes to fruit. You have likely heard that it's not great to let kids drink too much fruit juice. That's because fruit is high in sugar content. Juice lacks the fruit's fiber, which is essential for regulating the speed with which the fruit's sugars enter your bloodstream. This causes a spike in blood sugar, which is not a good thing (and you may be shocked to discover that some juices contain more sugar than soda).

Juice can be fattening. The reason again is the lack of fiber. Without fiber, it takes longer for you to feel full, and consequently you may wind up consuming more of the fruit than if you were eating them whole (as well as more of whatever food you also happen to be eating!).

MY VERDICT: Juice is a great way to pack a ton of vitamins and phytochemicals into a small beverage, and for people without weight and/or sugar management issues, it can be an easy, portable option for meeting your daily dose of fruits and vegetables.

Blending

When you blend fruits and vegetables, as you do in smoothies, you are consuming the entirety of the fruit or vegetable and getting the full digestive benefits of the dietary fiber. It's a nutritious way to fill up, so you will likely find yourself snacking less and staying sated until the next meal.

If you are partial to the consistency of juice and prefer a smoother texture to your smoothies, add more liquid and use a high-powered blender (which can be a total game-changer for making super creamy smoothies). While juicers remove the fiber from fruits and vegetables, blenders help to break down the fiber, not only in fruits and vegetables, but also in other ingredients like chia, hemp, flax seeds, and nuts.

That being said, it's important to pay attention to both the type and amount of fruit you put in your smoothies. Even with the fiber, an all-fruit smoothie can still cause a rise in blood sugar if it doesn't contain protein or fat. So balancing your smoothie with vegetables, nuts, and/or other sources of protein and fat is important, especially when it's serving as a meal.[2] I took this into consideration when developing the recipes for this book. Almost every smoothie—even the ones that feature only fruits (and no vegetables)—includes a fat and protein, and the handful that don't suggest super boosts that can provide them.

MY VERDICT: Smoothies are ideal vehicles for getting fruit into our bodies. Clearly I'm biased, but if you're looking to get your day started off right, and feel energized and sated till your next meal, then a well-balanced smoothie is the way to go!

2 . "Are Smoothies Better for You Than Juices?" The New York Times, 8.5.16

Smoothies Can Be Dessert

"Nice" creams, pops, and dessert smoothies are truly guilt-free confections, satisfying those sweet, creamy, and decadent cravings while also being nutritious. In fact, there are plenty of "nice" cream recipes that I prefer to the real thing. It's also great to be able to offer your kids dessert every night and feel great about it.

"Nice" Cream: To scratch my ice cream itch, I've become a big maker of "nice" cream, which totally satisfies my oversize ice cream urges in a nutritious way. "Nice" cream is a healthy take on ice cream, which is made in the blender using frozen bananas as the base. When blended, bananas simulate both the texture and creaminess of ice cream. Just add a variety of other fruits, superfoods, and a touch of liquid to create your desired flavor. Pureed smooth, it has a luscious frozen yogurt/gelato-like consistency that I find heavenly. The first time I made a "nice" cream and realized I could eat it as often as I liked was kind of up there with my wedding day and the births of my children.

You'll find "nice" cream recipes on pages 122 and 149, but any of the banana-based recipes in this book can be turned into a "nice" cream by adding an extra frozen banana to the blender and reducing the amount of liquid to about 2 to 3 tablespoons. Add the rest of your ingredients and turn on the blender. Use your blender's plunger (if it has one) to keep pushing the ingredients down into the spinning blade until everything becomes thick and whipped smooth. At this point you can eat it as is or freeze for one hour (and up to three) to give it even more of an ice cream–like consistency. If your blender doesn't have a plunger, you'll need to repeatedly turn off the blender, remove the lid, and scrape down the container's sides before blending again. While not essential, a strong blender with a plunger produces the best results, so if you're a "nice" cream addict like me, I highly recommend investing in one (check out page 38 for my blender picks).

Ice Pops: All of the recipes in this book can be turned into ice pops simply by pouring them into ice pop molds. I often double my morning smoothie recipe and divide it between glasses and ice pop molds, freezing the molds for at least four hours so my family can enjoy a treat any time of day.

Dessert Smoothies: Smoothies can also be a healthy way to end a meal, and there are plenty of recipes in this book that are perfect for dessert. You'll encounter most of them in the chapter called Decadent, as well as in the chapter on chocolate and vanilla flavors, but they're by no means limited to these recipes. Feel free to play around with your own favorite flavor combos. I find that you can satisfy almost any sweet craving by making a healthful version in your blender. Experiment and have fun.

SMOOTHIE HACK

Dairy-free or lactose intolerant but desire a thick and creamy smoothie? Try banana, avocado, frozen mango, frozen cauliflower, chia seeds, cashews, coconut milk, or dairy-free yogurt. (The lowest calorie options are cauliflower, chia seeds, and mango.)

Smoothies Appeal to Every Palate

Foods that are good for us don't always satisfy our taste cravings. But smoothies enable you to incorporate the most healthful ingredients deliciously, even if you don't love how they taste on their own.

The key is using ingredients with flavors you enjoy to dominate the taste of the smoothie. For example, for the veggie averse (my mother-in-law is one of them), I make smoothies that are very fruit forward in flavor, but still packed with veggies. Dark leafy greens like kale, spinach, and collard greens are some of the easiest ones to mask the flavor of with fruit, but this approach works with most vegetables. This strategy will produce smoothies that will appeal to almost any palate.

It's also easy to cover up the flavor of supplements that may not be enjoyable for you. I use vanilla, chocolate, nuts, and berries to hide the taste of my protein powder and collagen peptides.

No matter your palate, the adaptability of smoothies means it's easy to make them work for you.

"Picky" Eaters

Parents of picky eaters (a term readers of my first book know I don't like, but I'm using it here, as the meaning is universally understood) are constantly asking me how they can get their child to try smoothies. Feeding a child who is resistant to trying new things can feel daunting, provoke anxiety that your kid is not getting good nutrition, and cause unnecessary tension between parent and child. I go into the subject in more depth in my first book but know that it's important to first understand why kids become picky in the first place. There are a variety of factors at play, but for many children it's less about the food and more about control, especially with younger kids. Food is one of the easiest areas for them to successfully exert their will. By making your kids active participants in their meals, and bringing them into the entire process, from picking an ingredient at the store, to starting a window box garden, to helping make what they eat—rather than just putting their meals in front of them—you are empowering your child and giving them a way to exercise some control, and in turn have some ownership over what goes in their body. Because they're a fast, easy, and virtually mess-free cooking experience, smoothies are the perfect vehicle for doing this.

My printable Smoothie Planner is an easy to use, fun guide for making everyone the perfect smoothie. You can find it on the Weelicious website (https://weelicious.com/smoothie-project/). I have several laminated so I can give them to my kids with a dry erase marker and let them pick the things they want in their smoothie every day. But the planner is not just meant for kids. I find it to be an incredible resource for always reminding myself of the infinite possibilities for smoothie making.

Here are a few tips that have repeatedly worked with each of my three kids at different ages:

1. Ask your child what their favorite fruit is and create a simple smoothie with a vibrant color and fun name, like Pink Milk (page 126) or Green Monster (page 71).

2. When you're at the grocery store, offer your child the opportunity to pick any fruit or vegetable they want to try in their smoothie.

3. Come up with a smoothie based on your child's favorite flavor profile, and give them a choice of two vegetables to add.

4. Make a smoothie together. When kids have a hand in preparing their own food, chances are they will be more excited to try it.

5. Let your child name the smoothie. Kids love coming up with fun names for recipes, which makes them feel empowered.

6. Pick out a fun glass and/or straw with your child. Letting them have a designated smoothie container that's all theirs will make their smoothie feel even more special.

Making It Simple for Everyone
(Otherwise, What's the Point?)

We all know how important healthy eating is; however, the ability to accomplish more for others through constant connection to our jobs, responsibilities, and commitments has in many ways caused us to do less for ourselves.

That's why any roadmap for eating well has to be a) simple to incorporate, b) offer lots of variety, and c) be easy to maintain.

Smoothies deliver on all those fronts. This chapter puts simplicity front and center with guidance on how to make the most of your time and set you up for maximum success.

Prepping Smoothies: What to Do in Advance

If you're anything like me, you want to make smoothie prep as easy as possible. I created a few strategies to streamline my smoothie making that cut my prep time in half—maybe even more.

- Weekly Smoothie Prep: Just as I do for dinner prep, I create lists of the smoothies I want to make in the coming week and then make sure I have all the ingredients on hand. Earmark the recipes in this book that appeal most to you, and you can easily do the same.

- Smoothie Ingredient List: Keep a list of your smoothie ingredient staples on your phone or in your pantry so you always know what you need to buy the next time you are at the store. Help maintain your stock and save money by signing up for recurring product subscriptions on Thrive Market or Amazon.

- Smoothie Jars: One of my favorite smoothie prep strategies came by way of my husband, after he calculated how much time he was spending pulling out and measuring his dry ingredients every day. Line up five or six mason jars, one for each day of the week that you plan to have a smoothie, and put an equal amount of each dry ingredient (seeds, nuts, powders) in each jar. This is good to do on a weekend morning, or when you're not rushing to get out the door for work and school. It's a great system, especially if you are drinking the same smoothie every day or if your recipe requires a lot of dry ingredients. Just grab a mason jar from the fridge each morning and dump it in the blender with whatever fruit and veggies you have on hand. To see a fun video I made a while back of these being assembled, look on the Weelicious website under the title "Smoothie Jars" (https://weelicious.com/2017/11/30/smoothie-jars/).

• Smoothie Packs: Same idea as smoothie jars, only for fruit and vegetables. Pick your smoothie recipes for the week, portion the ingredients into airtight silicone zip-top bags, freezer bags, or quart containers, and place them in the freezer. Then all you need to do when you make your smoothie is dump the contents of one bag into the blender, add your liquid, and press the start button—sixty seconds total from the freezer to your tummy. That's just about the quickest healthy meal you can make. If you don't like your smoothies to be too cold, transfer a smoothie bag from the freezer to the fridge the night before to let the produce defrost overnight (I don't recommend combining your smoothie jars and packs into one container; it might seem more efficient, but in some cases the dry ingredients will start to interact and degrade and lose some of their nutritional potency).

Saving Your Smoothie for Later

As the mom of three, I'm all too aware how switching on a noisy blender at 6 a.m. and interrupting your family's precious sleep can be a problem. While a fresh smoothie is always best for maximum nutrient potency, it's still possible to make one ahead of time. After all, a smoothie that's been refrigerated overnight is still a better choice than grabbing a bagel with cream cheese.

Here are a few things to keep in mind:

• Immediately after making your smoothie, pour it into a glass container, seal tightly with an airtight, BPA-free lid, and transfer it to the refrigerator. Or, if you are taking it with you, put it in a dark insulated bag. Oxidization and light will degrade the nutrients in your smoothie.

• If you're prone to making poor dietary choices during the day, put together a double batch of your morning smoothie and store half of it in the fridge (or bring it with you in a dark insulated bag) so you can grab a quick and healthy choice whenever hunger strikes.

• Add a squeeze of lemon to your smoothie to keep the color bright (and add a boost of vitamin C).

• When you have some spare time on the weekend, whip up a huge batch of smoothies and divide them into mason jars, filling them three-quarters of the way up (this allows the smoothie to expand as it freezes and prevents the jar from cracking), and tightly seal with an airtight lid. You can freeze the smoothies for up to three months. Transfer a jar to the refrigerator the night before so it can defrost. In the morning, you'll be all ready to go. The ingredients usually will separate, which is totally normal, so give it a good shake before drinking. You can even replace the top with a mason jar lid fitted with a built-in straw hole that's perfect to bring on the go.

• If you make too much smoothie or for some reason can't drink what you made, try dividing it into ice pop molds and freezing overnight for a special treat (see page 24).

SMOOTHIE HACK

Too lazy to grab a knife and cutting board to slice bananas? Peel the banana and lightly push your pointer finger into the top. As you move your finger down, the banana will naturally separate into thirds lengthwise. Break the thirds into pieces and freeze.

Smoothie Organization

When bags and boxes of ingredients pile up on the shelves of your freezer, refrigerator, and pantry, things can get unsightly. Worse, it quickly becomes difficult to keep track of what ingredients you have (or have run out of). I can't tell you how many times I've run to the grocery to replenish my frozen raspberry supply only to discover I already had two bags stuffed in the back of my freezer (or how many times I've had all my ingredients in the blender except the one I've just realized that I'm out of). Keeping your ingredients organized makes living the Smoothie Project even easier. Here are my tips for each area of the kitchen.

FREEZER

- Mason jars are perfect for storing ingredients that you might not typically think to freeze. I transfer most of my smoothie ingredients, from bee pollen, hemp seeds, chia seeds, flax seeds, and wheat germ to nuts and seeds—even fresh dates—into tall, inexpensive glass mason jars that I label with a Sharpie and blue painter's tape and store on one shelf of the freezer door. This lets me easily see exactly what ingredients I have and extends their shelf life (i.e. chia seeds normally have a two-year shelf life that increases to four years in the freezer).

- Plastic shoe bins are great for organizing bags of frozen fruit. They help you maximize freezer space (and save on your energy bill, as you'll no longer find yourself keeping the freezer door open while you rummage through piled-up bags in search of the frozen blueberries). You can immediately see what you have, or you can pull the entire bin out and sort through it on the counter with the freezer door shut. You'll always know when it's time to restock, too. I use multiple boxes and label the front of each one with a Sharpie and blue painter's tape; this is especially helpful when you're storing a variety of different fruits in one bin—with one glance you'll always know exactly what's in it.

- Zip-top freezer bags are helpful to keep on hand. When fresh fruit and vegetables are starting to spot or become overripe, don't throw them away. Cut them into chunks, place the pieces on a parchment-lined baking sheet, freeze them overnight, and then place the frozen produce into the freezer bags. They'll stay fresh for up to four months. Eliminate those "how long has this stuff been in here" moments by labeling the bags with what's inside and the date you froze it.

Smoothie temperature can be an issue for some, especially during the winter. For example, if you live in Minnesota, the idea of drinking a smoothie in January when it's ten below may not be so enticing. Many of the smoothies in this book use room-temperature and refrigerated ingredients; however, for recipes that call for frozen fruit or veg, you can easily reduce the chill factor by placing your frozen ingredients in the refrigerator the night before so that they defrost overnight.

REFRIGERATOR

- With the exception of bananas, citrus, and persimmons, store most ripe fresh fruit and vegetables in the fridge until you're ready to use them (I let most fruit ripen on my counter and transfer it to the fridge when it's at my desired level of ripeness, but apples, berries, and grapes go right in the fridge). Never wash your produce until you're ready to consume it, as it can speed up formation of mold and cause certain fruits, in particular porous fruits like raspberries, to become waterlogged.

- Maximize the shelf life of fresh berries by removing them from their packaging and placing them in an airtight container lined top and bottom with paper towels (preferably a glass container and an unbleached paper towel). The paper towels help remove extra moisture, which can cause mold. You can take a similar approach with greens such as spinach, tatsoi, and kale: Place the cleaned, dry greens at the end of a long piece of paper towel, then roll it up. Place the roll in a zip-top bag and squeeze all the air out. The greens will keep for up to two weeks.

PANTRY

- Dedicate one shelf or drawer in your pantry to storing protein powders, probiotic powder, superfood powders, nuts, seeds, dried fruits, and more. If storing on a shelf, a basket or small lazy Susan can be particularly helpful for organizing everything neatly. When you can see everything at once, you'll find what you need quicker.

- If you're someone who goes to the supermarket frequently, you can rely on refrigerated milks, but if you go less often, shelf-stable milks are a good bet, as they keep for a long time—just make sure to refrigerate them after opening. Even if you primarily use refrigerated milk, never get caught without a liquid for your smoothie by keeping a few shelf-stable milks in the pantry. Coconut water, plant-based milk, even cow's milk all can be found in shelf-stable versions. For more on choosing liquids see page 246.

SMOOTHIE HACK

Want to avoid ever finding yourself without greens and fruits on hand? Powdered versions of greens and many superfruits like açaí, maqui, and pitaya will last for a long time in your pantry and are nutritionally potent. Many greens powders feature additional whole food ingredients such as probiotics and protein. Also check out my recipe for Green Cubes on page 84.

Tools of the Trade

Aside from a blender, making smoothies doesn't require special equipment. But if you are making them on a regular basis, investing in a few nice things can help make the process more efficient (and, dare I say, stylish). After exhaustive testing and research, here are some of my favorite tools for making and serving smoothies.

Blenders

The type of blender you choose is almost as important as the quality of the ingredients you put in it. Navigating the myriad brands and models in the marketplace can be overwhelming, which is why I've shared what to look for here.

Over the years, #smoothieproject followers occasionally message me to say that their kids won't drink their smoothies because the texture or taste isn't quite right, or that there are chunks and bits that won't pass through their straw. When I ask them what kind of blender are they using, without fail the answer is either a blender they've had for twenty years or a poorly made knockoff model. Luckily, blender technology has improved in recent years. More affordable models have stronger motors, making it possible to find a good blender for almost every budget.

You don't have to buy a top-of-the-line blender to be able to make silky smoothies. If you're like me and make at least a smoothie a day, it's can be worth spending a little extra for a powerful blender that can quickly puree the toughest of ingredients, but I've also used a number of reasonably priced blenders that turn out a super smooth smoothie.

Below are some of the features to consider when you're purchasing a blender:

Smoothie setting: Hardly essential, but if your primary reason for buying a blender is smoothies, this feature, designed for optimal pureeing, is pretty great.

Tamper/wand attachment: Super helpful for making "nice" cream (see page 24) and pushing particularly thick foods down into the blade.

Size: If you're only planning to make single-serve smoothies or have a small kitchen, you may want to consider a compact blender that's easy to store. But if you plan on making smoothies simultaneously for the whole family or large batches to freeze in individual jars for the future, a blender featuring a large-volume pitcher can be useful and a real time saver.

Model vs. price: Compare all of the models in your price range to see which one best suits your needs. Also read Amazon user reviews, ask friends, and compare outlets. For example, I've found several blenders on Amazon for up to $150 less than what it cost on the manufacturers' websites.

Noise: Blenders are loud by nature, so if you don't have time (or patience) to wait for everyone to be up before powering on your blender, look for one with a sound shield attachment (like a home version of what you might see on the blenders at a smoothie shop), which reduces the blender's noise level.

Some Blenders I Like

I've had my **KitchenAid Pro Line Series** ($499) for years and absolutely love it. It's pricey, but I use it more than any other appliance in my kitchen. And since I keep it on my counter all year long, it's nice that it's also beautiful to look at. It has a heavy-duty motor, which lets me puree whole nuts, seeds, dates, raw fruits, and vegetables into velvety drinks in a matter of seconds. The tamper, for pushing the ingredients into the blade to make "nice" cream, is essential for me. And the BPA-free thermal container is super easy to clean.

The **NutriBullet Balance** ($150) has a crazy powerful motor and is ideal for making two small smoothies or one large single-serve smoothie. The container you blend in doubles as your glass, and has a handy to-go lid. There's no need to measure your ingredients—it has a smart scale built into the base, which connects to an app on your phone. Just set the container on the base, type in the name of your ingredient, and keep adding it until you reach your desired calorie target. Great for calorie counters! Of all the higher end models listed here, it's the easiest on your wallet. My husband says his smoothies come out just as well as they do in our KitchenAid, which costs more than three times as much.

Ask any chef or foodie what their go-to blender brand is and the answer will almost inevitably be a Vitamix. When testing for and photographing this book, I used the **Vitamix Professional 750** ($598), which is a total workhorse with its variable speed control dial.

The **Blendtec Designer 725** ($450) can blend enough smoothies for four to six servings at a time and will pulverize the toughest of smoothie ingredients.

The newest kid on the blender block, the **Philips High Speed Connected Blender** ($399.95), with its powerful high-speed motor (up to 35,000 RPM) and noise-reducing dome, is truly impressive.

The **Breville Super Q** ($350) has a BPA-free lined jug and pre-programmed settings, at a slightly more affordable price than the other high-end blenders listed here—nice for those who want a strong blender with a softer price tag.

Five years ago, I bought my husband the **Ninja QB1004 Blender/Food Processor** ($28) to use as a travel blender for smoothies on the road. He also uses it at home to make nice cream. It comes with a handheld motor that fits on top of the included 48-ounce smoothie pitcher and 16-ounce chopper bowl. It doesn't puree as well as the other models listed here, but it's portable and you simply can't beat the price.

CARING FOR YOUR BLENDER

Caring for your blender is important for extending the life of your investment. If you "smoothie" every day, once a week you should:

1. Fill blender pitcher about halfway with hot tap water and add a teaspoon of dish soap.

2. Place pitcher on the base, cover with the top (if your blender's top is flimsy, place a towel on top to absorb any water that may leak out).

3. Turn on the blender and allow it to run for about 30 seconds.

4. Pour out the soapy water and rinse the pitcher with warm water until it's clean and clear.

5. For more stubborn stains resulting from long-term use, sprinkle baking soda on a sponge soaked with a little white vinegar and scrub the interior until the stains begin to disappear. Clean carefully near the bottom or remove the blade to clean separately.

Cups and Straws

Plastic has been known to leach into the food it has contact with, so I avoid drinking out of plastic straws and containers and favor products made of glass, stainless steel, or silicone.

Most days I drink my smoothie from tall glasses bought from IKEA. They're nothing fancy, but they look super chic with the right straw. The glass straws I use—I like Simply Straws and Hummingbird—are very thick, incredibly durable, environmentally friendly, and easy to clean. Stainless steel straws are also great options, especially when traveling, and 100 percent food safe (many smoothie travel/to-go cups now come with one). Finally, there are a lot of good silicone straws as well as durable paper straws, many of which come in fun patterns and are a better choice for the environment than plastic.

When it comes to travel cups, there are endless brands to choose from online. I prefer ones from S'well and Yeti, but there are plenty of good options.

tropical

Mango Spice

Serves 1

Ingredients:

¾ cup (120 g) frozen mango chunks

½ fresh or frozen banana, peeled

¼ cup (33 g) frozen cauliflower florets

1 teaspoon unrefined coconut oil

¼ teaspoon ground turmeric

¼ teaspoon ground cinnamon

1 pinch freshly ground black pepper

1 tablespoon hemp seeds

1 cup (240 ml) almond milk or milk of choice

Combine all the ingredients in a blender and blend until smooth.

OPTIONAL SUPER BOOSTS:

BEE POLLEN

CHIA SEEDS

FLAX SEEDS

MACA POWDER

VANILLA OR PLAIN PROTEIN POWDER

COLLAGEN PEPTIDES

MCT OIL

REISHI

ASHWAGANDHA

PROBIOTIC POWDER

Smoothies with tropical flavors can whisk your taste buds to a far-off place where life is easy, all while doing the inside of your body good (you won't get any sand in your bathing suit either).

Flavors like mango, pineapple, and coconut all evoke images of being on an island with palm trees swaying in the wind, but so too can certain spices.

Spices have truly magical and warming Ayurvedic properties, which, as I discovered, can really brighten the flavor of smoothies. Years ago, I was given a spice blend by an Indian woman I met at a health conference; when she suggested that I add it to a smoothie, I was a bit taken aback. I had never thought to do that before, but when I did, my mind was blown. The flavors of the cinnamon, turmeric, and even the crack of pepper do double duty, beautifully complementing the sweet mango and banana while also aiding digestion and combating inflammation in your body. Since I started making this, it has become one of my family's most-requested smoothies. I prefer to use unrefined coconut oil, as it offers a nice coconut flavor, but you can use refined instead for a more neutral taste.

Dragon

Serves 1

Ingredients:

½ cup (50 g) frozen or fresh dragon fruit

1 fresh or frozen banana, peeled

¼ cup (33 g) frozen cauliflower florets

1 serving collagen peptides

1 serving vanilla protein powder

¾ cup (180 ml) milk of choice

Combine all the ingredients in a blender and blend until smooth.

OPTIONAL SUPER BOOSTS:

BEE POLLEN

HEMP SEEDS

FLAX SEEDS

MACA POWDER

REISHI

ASHWAGANDHA

This beautiful smoothie gets its name from the main ingredient, pitaya, also known as dragon fruit. The first time I encountered dragon fruit was about ten years ago at my local farmers' market. The farmer selling it had cut several in half to showcase the variety of colors they come in: purple-red, pink, white, and yellow, the flesh speckled with tiny black seeds. I was mesmerized not only by the vibrancy of the flesh, but also by its mild tropical flavor. Years later, the bright pink variety started popping up in frozen food sections throughout the country, making it easy to bring a bit of exoticism to your smoothies.

Dragon fruit is low in calories but filling, high in vitamin C, and, yes, mesmerizing to look at. If you're trying to cap your calories, you can sub more dragon fruit for half of the banana—which also will make the color of the smoothie even brighter.

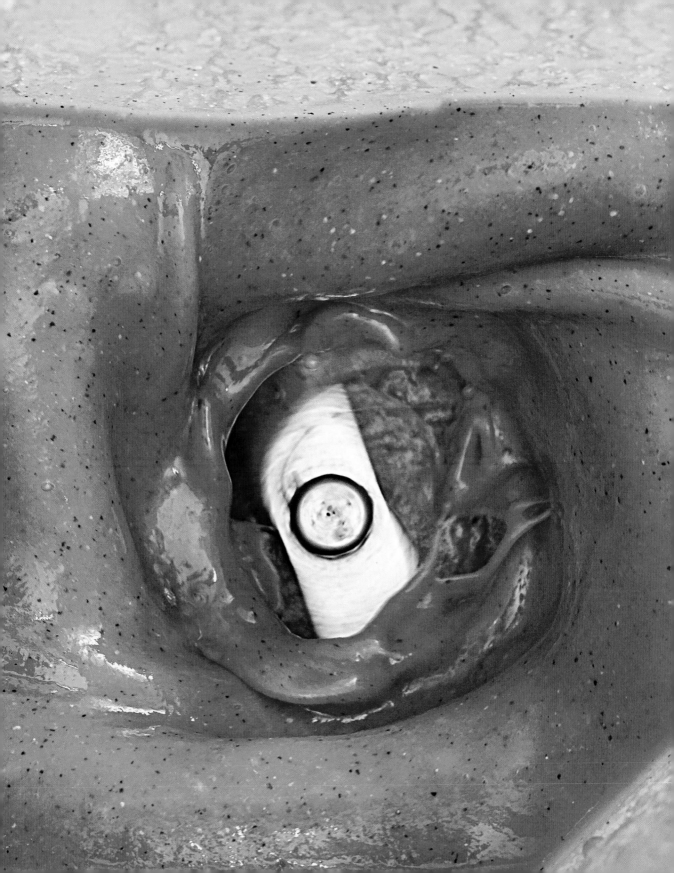

Secret Mango Creamsicle

Serves 1

Ingredients:

½ cup (80 g) frozen mango chunks

½ ripe persimmon (Hachiya or Fuyu), stemmed

1 small carrot, peeled and chopped
(about ¼ cup/32 g)

1 tablespoon almond butter

1 teaspoon flax seeds or flaxseed meal

1 teaspoon hemp seeds

¼ teaspoon ground cinnamon or favorite
spice blend

1 cup (240 ml) coconut milk beverage or
almond milk, or milk of choice

**Combine all the ingredients in a blender
and blend until smooth.**

OPTIONAL SUPER BOOSTS:

BEE POLLEN

COLLAGEN PEPTIDES

MACA POWDER

REISHI

ASHWAGANDHA

You might not be able to put your finger on what makes this smoothie unique, but you'll want to keep drinking it over and over again. The secret ingredient is persimmon, which provides sweetness and creaminess while letting the mango flavor shine through. This smoothie tastes like the freshest, healthiest Creamsicle you've ever had.

If you've never tried a persimmon before, I insist you hunt one down when they're in season. They are both delicious and a game-changing ingredient in smoothie making. Persimmons are known for their sweet, honey-like flavor and the wildly divergent textures of the two main varieties. Fuyu persimmons resemble apples in both shape and the crispness of their flesh, while Hachiya persimmons are more oblong and their flesh has a delicate, creamy, jelly-like consistency, which makes them perfect for eating with a spoon—or, even better, putting in your smoothies. Fuyus are great for smoothies, too, but no matter which variety you pick, make sure that they're super ripe before going in the blender.

There's plenty of protein in this smoothie from the almond butter and hemp seeds and a boost of fiber from the fruit, veg, and flax.

Piña Colada

Serves 1

Ingredients:

½ fresh or frozen banana, peeled

½ cup (80 g) fresh or frozen pineapple chunks

¼ cup (33 g) frozen cauliflower florets

¾ cup (180 ml) coconut milk or milk of choice

1 tablespoon hemp seeds

1 serving collagen peptides

1 handful ice

Combine all the ingredients in a blender and blend until smooth.

OPTIONAL SUPER BOOSTS:

BEE POLLEN

CHIA SEEDS

FLAX SEEDS

VANILLA OR PLAIN PROTEIN POWDER

SPIRULINA

CHLORELLA

REISHI

ASHWAGANDHA

PROBIOTIC POWDER

GREENS POWDER

GOJI BERRIES

MACA POWDER

PINK HIMALAYAN SALT

BRAZIL NUTS

Raise your hand if you're ready for a vacation! While jetting off to Tahiti may not be in the cards, this piña colada smoothie can feel like the next best thing. I love how the subtle tartness of refreshing pineapple intertwines with the silky-sweet creaminess of coconut milk. You can use canned coconut milk (light or whole, if you're feeling decadent) or a refrigerated coconut milk beverage, which has a lighter taste. To make mine even creamier (without seriously impacting the calories), I add frozen cauliflower, which has a neutral flavor that doesn't affect the taste of this smoothie at all. It also adds a vegetable to the mix—hooray! If you want to really go crazy, you can give it a shot of rum. Adults only, of course.

Pineapple Matcha

Serves 1

Ingredients:

¾ cup (120 g) frozen pineapple chunks

2 fresh kale leaves, thick stems removed, chopped

½ teaspoon matcha powder

1 serving vanilla protein powder

¾ cup (180 ml) milk of choice

Combine all the ingredients in a blender and blend until smooth.

OPTIONAL SUPER BOOSTS:

BEE POLLEN

CHIA SEEDS

HEMP SEEDS

COLLAGEN PEPTIDES

REISHI

ASHWAGANDHA

PROBIOTIC POWDER

GOJI BERRIES

PINK HIMALAYAN SALT

BRAZIL NUTS

I've never seen anyone take as much joy from finding and cutting the perfect pineapple as my mother-in-law does. She's such a pineapple connoisseur, in fact, that she can tell exactly how sweet it will be just by smelling and touching it. (If it smells sweet and fragrant and you can gently pull out one of the green leaves at the top, you've got a winner.)

So I tip my hat to my MIL with this predominantly pineapple smoothie, which includes a handful of nutrient- and fiber-packed greens to add to its beautiful green color. It's the perfect smoothie for anyone attached to their morning cup of joe, as antioxidant-rich matcha gives a boost that rivals coffee. I love it with vanilla protein powder, but you can use any flavor protein powder you enjoy.

Passion

Serves 1

Ingredients:

1 cup (160 g) fresh or frozen mango chunks

2 passion fruits*

½ cup (66 g) frozen cauliflower florets

1 serving collagen peptides

½ cup (120 ml) coconut water or coconut milk

Combine all the ingredients in a blender and blend until smooth.

Scoop out the fruit from the rind with a spoon and add to your smoothie, seeds and all. If you don't have a high-powered blender, press the fruit through a sieve and use only the juice.

OPTIONAL SUPER BOOSTS:

BEE POLLEN

CHIA SEEDS

HEMP SEEDS

FLAX SEEDS

MACA POWDER

VANILLA OR PLAIN PROTEIN POWDER

MCT OIL

PROBIOTIC POWDER

GOJI BERRIES

AÇAÍ POWDER

PINK HIMALAYAN SALT

BRAZIL NUTS

Years ago, I bought an organic passion fruit vine for twenty dollars at the farmers' market. I planted it and forgot about it until the day I noticed the most magical blossoms crawling through our bushes. Much to my surprise, within weeks it had produced one hundred or so passion fruit. Years later, that once little vine has climbed a tree, snaking around the branches and producing almost ten times the amount of fruits it did that first season. Every morning before I get in the car, I collect a basketful of the fruits that have plummeted to the ground. My whole family knows to be cautious during passion fruit season, because if you don't watch out, they'll bop you on the head.

If you've never had a passion fruit, I urge you to try one. They're spectacular, possessing a truly intense, complex tropical flavor, with the satisfyingly crunchy edible seeds complementing the tart sweetness of the pulpy fruit. They add a boost of fiber and a taste you'll never forget.

On Vacation

Serves 1

Ingredients:

½ cup (80 g) frozen mango chunks

½ cup (80 g) frozen pineapple chunks

¼ cup (35 g) peeled, seeded, and chopped papaya

¼ cup (33 g) frozen cauliflower florets

1 tablespoon cashew butter or 5 cashews raw, unsalted*

¾ cup (180 ml) coconut milk

Combine all the ingredients in a blender and blend until smooth.

*If you don't have a high-powered blender, soak the cashews overnight (and discard the water before using) to make them easier to puree perfectly smooth (see page 249).

OPTIONAL SUPER BOOSTS:

BEE POLLEN

HEMP SEEDS

COLLAGEN PEPTIDES

MCT OIL

REISHI

ASHWAGANDHA

I remember being at the beach as a kid, dreaming of the day I'd be old enough to have one of those tall drinks adorned with a fancy umbrella to sip on as I sat in the sand with my toes in the warm water. Even though I'm an adult now, I still dream about those drinks, because for parents, going to the beach pretty much consists of arguments about applying sunscreen, intermittent bursts of panic thinking you've lost a child, and trying to keep sand out of your iPhone.

Whenever I want to recapture the pre-kids feeling of being on the beach, I make this smoothie. It's as close to paradise as you can possibly get while living the daily grind. The coconut milk makes it light, cool, and refreshing but also filling. If you're watching your calories but still want the protein, substitute a scoop of your favorite protein powder for the cashew butter.

Pure Gold

Serves 1

Ingredients:

¾ cup (120 g) frozen mango chunks

½-inch (1.25-cm) piece fresh turmeric, peeled, or ¼ teaspoon ground turmeric

1 pinch freshly ground black pepper

1 pinch cayenne (optional)

1 tablespoon coconut, MCT, or XTC oil

¼ teaspoon lime zest

2 teaspoons fresh lime juice

1 cup (240 ml) coconut water

Combine all the ingredients in a blender and blend until smooth.

OPTIONAL SUPER BOOSTS:

BEE POLLEN

CHIA SEEDS

HEMP SEEDS

VANILLA OR PLAIN PROTEIN POWDER

COLLAGEN PEPTIDES

REISHI

ASHWAGANDHA

Take one sip of Pure Gold and you'll swear you can feel the golden sun shining in your belly. It has a deep mango flavor and will fill you up in spite of its light taste. This smoothie is incredibly hydrating from the coconut water (which also replenishes electrolytes), and the addition of turmeric can help combat inflammation (the fat in the coconut oil and crack of black pepper enhances absorption and potency).

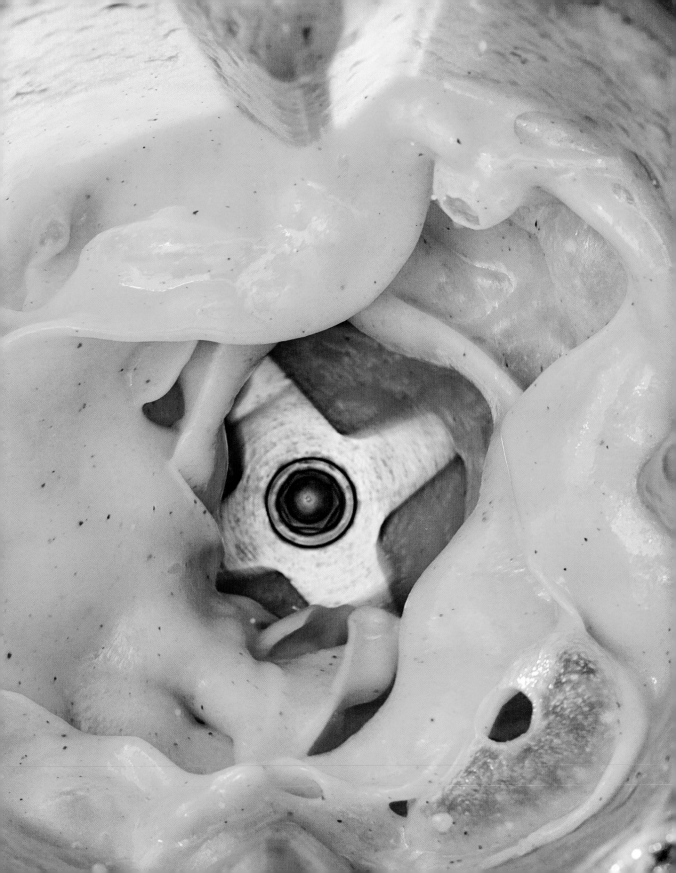

Lassi is an Indian yogurt drink often blended with spices

Tropical Lassi

Serves 1

Ingredients:

½ cup (74 g) fresh or frozen blueberries

½ cup (80 g) frozen mango chunks

¼ teaspoon lime zest

½ cup (120 ml) plain or vanilla yogurt

2 teaspoons honey, or more to taste

6 almonds, or 1 tablespoon almond butter

¾ cup (180 ml) milk of choice

1 handful ice

⅛ teaspoon ground cinnamon (optional)

Combine all the ingredients in a blender and blend until smooth.

OPTIONAL SUPER BOOSTS:

BEE POLLEN

CHIA SEEDS

HEMP SEEDS

FLAX SEEDS

MACA POWDER

VANILLA OR PLAIN PROTEIN POWDER

COLLAGEN PEPTIDES

MCT OIL

REISHI

ASHWAGANDHA

PROBIOTIC POWDER

GOJI BERRIES

CAMU CAMU POWDER

PINK HIMALAYAN SALT

BRAZIL NUTS

Lassi is an Indian yogurt drink often blended with spices. I dream of the day I can visit India and have a real lassi there, but until then I'll take a tall glass of this. A lassi technically is not a smoothie, but with the addition of milk it can certainly pass for one. The probiotic power of yogurt forms the base of this recipe, and it's mixed with tropical mango and tart blueberries, which give the drink its bright blue color.

green

Avo-Coco Kale

Serves 1

Ingredients:

½ ripe avocado, pitted and peeled

½ cup (50 g) frozen coconut sheets or chunks

2 fresh kale leaves, thick stems removed, chopped

1 dried date, pitted

1 teaspoon fresh lime juice

1 cup (240 ml) milk of choice

1 handful ice

Combine all the ingredients in a blender and blend until smooth.

OPTIONAL SUPER BOOSTS:

BEE POLLEN

CHIA SEEDS

HEMP SEEDS

FLAX SEEDS

MACA POWDER

VANILLA OR PLAIN PROTEIN POWDER

COLLAGEN PEPTIDES

SPIRULINA

CHLORELLA

REISHI

ASHWAGANDHA

PROBIOTIC POWDER

PINK HIMALAYAN SALT

BRAZIL NUTS

Green smoothies can be the pinnacle of health. I personally don't like mine to taste too "green," so my green smoothie recipes have a sweet element to balance things out and make sure they deliver maximum deliciousness. Case in point is this Avo-Coco Kale smoothie.

I give my oldest daughter full credit for this ingredient combination. Two of her favorite foods are avocado and coconut, and while she's a true omnivore, she's quite specific when it comes to what she wants in her smoothie. She prefers me to make this one with less almond milk and pour it in a bowl so she can eat it with a spoon. I, on the other hand, love it just as the recipe directs. Either way it's super satisfying, but I figure since I wrote the book, I get to decide which version of the recipe goes in it!

Avocado Greens

Serves 1

Ingredients:

½ ripe avocado, pitted and peeled

½ frozen banana, peeled

2 fresh kale leaves, thick stems removed, chopped

1 serving vanilla protein powder

1 tablespoon chia seeds

¾ cup (180 ml) milk of choice

2 ice cubes

Combine all the ingredients in a blender and blend until smooth.

OPTIONAL SUPER BOOSTS:

BEE POLLEN

HEMP SEEDS

FLAX SEEDS

MACA POWDER

COLLAGEN PEPTIDES

REISHI

ASHWAGANDHA

In my early years modeling, when I didn't know better about good nutrition, at times I fell prey to no-fat and low-fat fad diets, which basically left me feeling nothing but hungry. Our bodies need fats. They're an energy source, aid in vitamin absorption, and help our nervous systems to function properly. All fat is not created equal, though. It's important to avoid saturated fats and focus on monounsaturated fats such as those found in nuts, seeds, and especially avocados. I don't think a day goes by that I don't eat at least half an avocado. While avocados are delicious added to salads, in guacamole, and mashed on toast, they also happen to be a secret, magical ingredient for smoothies, as they lend a scrumptious taste and creamy texture.

Avocado Shake

Serves 1

Ingredients:

½ ripe avocado, pitted and peeled

½ fresh or frozen banana, peeled

1 large handful ice

¾ cup (180 ml) milk of choice

2 to 3 teaspoons honey, or to taste

Combine all the ingredients in a blender and blend until smooth.

OPTIONAL SUPER BOOSTS:

BEE POLLEN

HEMP SEEDS

CHIA SEEDS

FLAX SEEDS

MACA POWDER

COLLAGEN PEPTIDES

REISHI

ASHWAGANDHA

I have a friend from Brazil who is passionate about food. Growing up, she had a huge avocado tree in her backyard, and she and her family used to eat them straight out of the shell or use them to make sweet treats. In the United States, avocado is generally used in savory dishes, but in Brazil it's mainly used in sweet things—it is a fruit, after all.

When I started making this avocado shake, it was a revelation. It's incredibly creamy and addictive and contains heart-healthy monounsaturated fatty acids and fiber. It's a simple, straightforward treat that's poured out of our blender all avocado season long.

Bright Green

Serves 1

Ingredients:

1 cup (30 g) fresh spinach

½ fresh or frozen banana, peeled

¼ cup (40 g) fresh or frozen pineapple chunks

½ cup (80 g) frozen mango chunks

¾ cup (180 ml) orange juice

Combine all the ingredients in a blender and blend until smooth.

OPTIONAL SUPER BOOSTS:

BEE POLLEN

HEMP SEEDS

COLLAGEN PEPTIDES

The first time I made this smoothie was for my son's kindergarten class on St. Patrick's Day. I had been asked by his teacher to make something bright green that didn't contain any artificial food dyes for the kids to eat. I figured a smoothie would be fun and easy for five-year-olds, but I knew that my biggest challenge was going to be the color itself.

I employed a couple of clever tactics. First was having them make the smoothies with me—if you get kids involved, they're much more likely to want to try the food. The second was using spinach. Spinach has a neutral flavor, so most foods you mix with it will overpower any potential "green" taste. I chose banana, pineapple, mango, and orange juice to give it a naturally sweet, almost tropical flavor. The goal was to make something that looked green but didn't taste green.

It worked. Watching all the kids making and enjoying this smoothie—right down to them cheers-ing each other's glasses—made my heart explode. Almost as great was the messages I received from parents to say their kids told them they had spinach at school that day—and liked it!

Chai Beauty Greens

Serves 1

Ingredients:

1½ cups (45 g) fresh spinach

¼ teaspoon fresh ginger, peeled and sliced (optional)

1 serving vanilla protein powder

1 serving collagen peptides

1 tablespoon chia seeds

½ teaspoon chai spices (or mix of cinnamon, ground ginger, nutmeg, and cloves)

1 cup (240 ml) almond milk or milk of choice

1 handful ice

Combine all the ingredients in a blender and blend until smooth.

OPTIONAL SUPER BOOSTS:

BEE POLLEN

HEMP SEEDS

FLAX SEEDS

MACA POWDER

MCT OIL

REISHI

ASHWAGANDHA

Whenever I drink this smoothie I feel like I'm doing so many good things for my body. The collagen peptides help strengthen my hair, skin, and nails. The chia seeds are rich in omega-3 fatty acids, which support brain function (and help me stay full until lunch), and the spinach is high in insoluble fiber and packed with so many important vitamins and nutrients. The chai spices (my favorite is a combination of cinnamon, ginger, nutmeg, and cloves) aid digestion and have a warming effect in your body. This one is for anyone who wants a low-sugar smoothie that makes you glow from head to toe.

Green Goddess

Serves 1

Ingredients:

1 frozen banana, peeled

1 dried date, pitted

1 tablespoon almond butter

1 serving chocolate protein powder*

1 tablespoon chlorella

1 serving collagen peptides

1 cup (240 ml) almond milk or milk of choice

Combine all the ingredients in a blender and blend until smooth.

For a deeper chocolate flavor, replace the chocolate protein powder with 2 teaspoons cacao powder.

OPTIONAL SUPER BOOSTS:

BEE POLLEN

CHIA SEEDS

HEMP SEEDS

FLAX SEEDS

REISHI

ASHWAGANDHA

PROBIOTIC POWDER

PINK HIMALAYAN SALT

BRAZIL NUTS

Want to feel like a goddess every day? Your body is a temple, so at the very least shouldn't you be the high priestess? This smoothie is a great step toward feeling your best all day long. First, the vibrant green color makes you feel better just looking at it. The taste, though, may surprise you. In spite of its verdant color, it has a luscious, deep chocolate and almond flavor, which completely masks the mild taste of the chlorella, a nutrient-rich single-celled green algae that's chockablock with vitamins, minerals, antioxidants, and omega-3 fatty acids to help boost your immune system, lower cholesterol, keep blood pressure in check, and much more. No matter your age, this smoothie will fill you up with that goddess vibe. It's absolutely scrumptious.

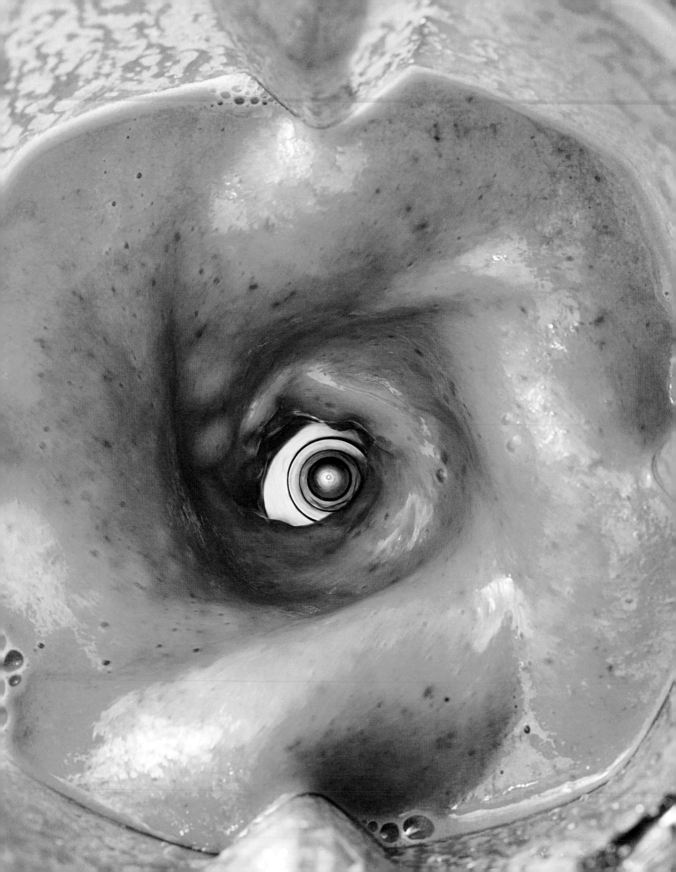

Green Monster

Serves 1

Ingredients:

1 frozen banana, peeled

1½ cups (45 g) fresh spinach

1 tablespoon almond or peanut butter

1 cup (240 ml) milk of choice

Combine all the ingredients in a blender and blend until smooth.

OPTIONAL SUPER BOOSTS:

BEE POLLEN

CHIA SEEDS

HEMP SEEDS

VANILLA OR PLAIN PROTEIN POWDER

COLLAGEN PEPTIDES

REISHI

ASHWAGANDHA

PROBIOTIC POWDER

PINK HIMALAYAN SALT

BRAZIL NUTS

When my oldest daughter was three years old and just starting to get into smoothies, we would make this one together. I'd allow her to pack in as many greens as possible, which she found fun, and it also gave her control of what kind of good things went into her body. Its name came simply from the color and her imagination.

I call this one a gateway smoothie, as it's perfect for first-timers to start with. It uses just four ingredients but tastes like you made it with a lot more, and it packs a massive nutritional punch of iron and fiber. For little ones wary of drinking anything green, assure them it doesn't taste that way. All they'll taste is the sweet banana and savory nut butter wrapped in a ton of love.

Super Greens

Serves 1

Ingredients:

2 fresh kale leaves, thick stems removed, chopped

¼ cup (25 g) chopped celery

½ Persian cucumber, unpeeled and chopped or ¼ English cucumber, peeled and chopped

¼ cup (40 g) frozen pineapple chunks

¼ lemon (with peel and pith), seeds removed

½ Gala, Fuji, or other sweet apple, cored, seeded, and cut into chunks*

1-inch (2.5-cm) piece fresh ginger, peeled

2 sprigs fresh mint leaves

½ cup (120 ml) coconut water, water, or herbal tea

Combine all the ingredients in a blender and blend until smooth.

If you don't have a high-powered blender, peel the apple.

OPTIONAL SUPER BOOSTS:

COLLAGEN PEPTIDES

PROBIOTIC POWDER

PINK HIMALAYAN SALT

GOLDEN BERRIES

My in-laws visit us often, and whenever they're here, without fail we eat at Le Pain Quotidien at least twice. We all have our favorites there, but everyone loves their Super Greens Smoothie. It's served with a frothy foam on the top, and the second it's set in front of me I take my straw and immediately suck it down. I fell so in love with that smoothie that I needed to figure out how to make it at home.

It took me some time to get the ratios just right, but eventually I think I nailed it. The secret ingredient is the fresh mint, which takes the taste to a whole new level, and the key to re-creating the foam and taste of the smoothie is leaving the peel on the lemon and apple. Now I don't have to wait for my in-laws to visit to enjoy this beauty again—I can just make it at home!

Sweet Green

Serves 1

Ingredients:

½ Persian cucumber, unpeeled and chopped or ¼ English cucumber, peeled and chopped*

½ kiwi, with skin

½ cup (15 g) fresh spinach

1 dried date, pitted

1 serving hemp or vanilla protein powder

1 tablespoon chia seeds

1 tablespoon almond butter

1 cup (240 ml) almond milk, coconut water, or milk of choice

Combine all the ingredients in a blender and blend until smooth.

If you're using English cucumber, peel it; Persian cucumber needs no peeling.

OPTIONAL SUPER BOOSTS:

BEE POLLEN

HEMP SEEDS

FLAX SEEDS

COLLAGEN PEPTIDES

REISHI

ASHWAGANDHA

PROBIOTIC POWDER

PINK HIMALAYAN SALT

BRAZIL NUTS

When I was a little girl, I would accompany my mom on her weekly grocery runs. I'd sit in the cart as she wheeled me around letting me sample different foods. Those trips helped me fall in love with a wide variety of foods, and kiwi was one of them. I remember my mother telling me how exotic and rare it was, especially in Kentucky, so of course that made me crave it even more.

Kiwi is incredibly high in vitamin C, which can help with skin health and lower blood pressure. Its fuzzy skin triples the fiber intake of the flesh, preserves much of the vitamin C content, and has no taste, so don't peel it off. If you're not a fan of green smoothies, give this sweet green one a try.

Triple Green

Ingredients:

2 fresh kale leaves, thick stems removed, chopped

½ cup (15 g) fresh spinach

¼ cup (23 g) fresh or frozen broccoli florets, or ¼ ripe avocado, pitted and peeled

1 frozen banana, peeled

1 dried date, pitted

1 tablespoon cashew butter, or 4 cashews raw, unsalted*

¾ cup (180 ml) milk of choice

Combine all the ingredients in a blender and blend until smooth.

*If you don't have a high-powered blender, soak the cashews overnight (and discard the water before using) to make them easier to puree perfectly smooth (see page 249).

OPTIONAL SUPER BOOSTS:

BEE POLLEN

CHIA SEEDS

HEMP SEEDS

FLAX SEEDS

VANILLA OR PLAIN PROTEIN POWDER

COLLAGEN PEPTIDES

REISHI

ASHWAGANDHA

PROBIOTIC POWDER

GOJI BERRIES

PINK HIMALAYAN SALT

BRAZIL NUTS

Can you put too many greens in your smoothie? Not in my book. Kale, spinach, and broccoli are a trifecta of nutrition in this smoothie, as they're high in fiber, which keeps your digestion running smoothly and also helps you to absorb all the vitamins you're getting. If you can get three varieties of greens in your body by breakfast, you have already won the day.

This smoothie is basically a salad in a glass, only better, as it's pureed and naturally easier to digest. To cut out any bitter flavor, I add natural sweetness from banana and date, plus cashews for protein. If you don't like broccoli, avocado is a good substitute and will make this even creamier. You can easily add vanilla or chocolate protein powder for additional flavor.

Our whole family loves this smoothie

Vanilla Kale Spirulina

Serves 1

Ingredients:

2 fresh kale leaves, thick stems removed, chopped

½ frozen banana, peeled

1 teaspoon spirulina

1 tablespoon hemp seeds

2 dried dates, pitted

¼ teaspoon vanilla extract or ⅛ teaspoon vanilla paste

¾ cup (180 ml) milk of choice

1 handful ice

Combine all the ingredients in a blender and blend until smooth.

OPTIONAL SUPER BOOSTS:

BEE POLLEN

CHIA SEEDS

FLAX SEEDS

MACA POWDER

VANILLA OR PLAIN PROTEIN POWDER

COLLAGEN PEPTIDES

MCT OIL

REISHI

ASHWAGANDHA

PROBIOTIC POWDER

PINK HIMALAYAN SALT

BRAZIL NUTS

Our whole family loves this smoothie. It's loaded with omega-3 fatty acids, fiber, and vitamins K, A, and C, but the reason we make it over and over again is the taste. Plus I'm a big fan of spirulina. It has a vibrant blue-green color, is nutrient dense, and has significant antioxidant and anti-inflammatory effects.

Green Sunshine

Serves 1

Ingredients:

1 small ripe avocado, pitted and peeled

½ cup (80 g) fresh or frozen pineapple chunks

2 fresh kale leaves, thick stems removed, chopped, or 1 serving greens powder

¼ cup (25 g) frozen coconut sheets or chunks

2 teaspoons fresh lime juice

¾ cup (180 ml) coconut water

Combine all the ingredients in a blender and blend until smooth.

OPTIONAL SUPER BOOSTS:

BEE POLLEN

HEMP SEEDS

CHIA SEEDS

COLLAGEN PEPTIDES

VANILLA PROTEIN POWDER

CHLORELLA

SPIRULINA

HEMP SEEDS

MCT OIL

REISHI

ASHWAGANDHA

CHAGA

When you're trying to keep you blood sugar in check, it's important to be mindful of the types of fruit you add to your smoothies. This one is a great option, as it's made with low-sugar fruits: avocado, which is packed with more than twenty vitamins and minerals; pineapple for a touch of sweetness; and coconut meat. A handful of kale gives it color and added iron and fiber. When these ingredients are combined, you get my take on the classic tropical piña colada, only this one is bright green.

Creamy Kale

Serves 1

Ingredients:

3 fresh kale leaves, thick stems removed, chopped

1 frozen banana, peeled

¼ cup (30 g) cashews raw, unsalted*

2 dried dates, pitted

¼ teaspoon vanilla extract or ⅛ teaspoon vanilla paste

1 serving collagen peptides

½ cup (120 ml) milk of choice

1 handful ice

OPTIONAL SUPER BOOSTS:

BEE POLLEN

CHIA SEEDS

HEMP SEEDS

FLAX SEEDS

VANILLA OR PLAIN PROTEIN POWDER

REISHI

ASHWAGANDHA

PROBIOTIC POWDER

PINK HIMALAYAN SALT

BRAZIL NUTS

Combine all the ingredients in a blender and blend until smooth.

*If you don't have a high-powered blender, soak the cashews overnight (and discard the water before using) to make them easier to puree perfectly smooth (see page 249).

We all know those people who hate eating kale (or oftentimes any greens, for that matter). One of them just might be living with you. My son, for one, didn't want any greens in his smoothies when I started him on the Smoothie Project, but I had a trick up my sleeve, one I hope you'll try employing as well. Play a little game: have them close their eyes and take a sip, then ask them what it tastes like. I promise they'll never guess that it has kale inside. Sweet dates, banana, and cashews give it a flavor akin to a creamy vanilla shake, and it has a thick, almost soft-serve texture that will win over even the grumpiest greens grouch.

Green Cubes

Ingredients:

1 cup (30 g) fresh spinach

4 fresh kale leaves, thick stems removed, chopped

1 fresh or frozen banana, peeled

1 cup (240 ml) milk of choice, coconut water, or water

Combine all the ingredients in a blender and blend until smooth. Pour the mixture into ice cubes trays and freeze overnight. Transfer the cubes to a freezer bag or container and store in the freezer for up to 4 months.

How often do you forget to buy fresh greens at the market and then find yourself out of luck when you set out to make a green smoothie? Or what about the times you go to the fridge to grab your greens only to find them totally wilted?

I started making these cubes a few years ago, and they were an instant game changer. I simply add two cubes to any smoothie recipe in place of ½ cup (15 g) of fresh greens. The banana lends a touch of sweetness, but you can leave it out if you are a greens purest. You can pop these into any smoothie recipe in this book for added green goodness.

vanilla +
chocolate +
coffee +
matcha

Vanilla Cinnamon Date Shake

Serves 1

Ingredients:

1 fresh or frozen banana, peeled

¼ cup (33 g) frozen cauliflower florets

2 dried dates, pitted

¼ teaspoon ground cinnamon

¼ teaspoon vanilla extract or ⅛ teaspoon vanilla paste

1 tablespoon hemp seeds

1 tablespoon almond butter

1 tablespoon flax seeds or flaxseed meal

¾ cup (180 ml) almond milk or milk of choice

Combine all the ingredients in a blender and blend until smooth.

OPTIONAL SUPER BOOSTS:

BEE POLLEN

CHIA SEEDS

MACA POWDER

VANILLA OR PLAIN PROTEIN POWDER

COLLAGEN PEPTIDES

MCT OIL

REISHI

ASHWAGANDHA

PINK HIMALAYAN SALT

BRAZIL NUTS

Shortly after starting the Smoothie Project, I realized that for years I had been asking my kids to go to school every morning fired up and ready to perform while filling their tanks with bread, pancakes, waffles, and other wheat- and dairy-heavy breakfast items that likely only aided them in doing the opposite. Something had to change, but I didn't want them to feel deprived of their favorite flavors and foods. On the days that they're craving our breakfasts of yore, I'll make them this shake that tastes reminiscent of Cinnamon Toast Crunch Cereal. Top it with a handful of cereal or granola and you'll be a real hero!

Awake

Ingredients:

½ cup (120 ml) cold brew or your favorite strong-brewed coffee

2 teaspoons grass-fed butter (if lactose intolerant, substitute ghee)

1 teaspoon MCT oil

1 serving collagen peptides

½ teaspoon maca powder

⅛ teaspoon ground cinnamon

½ cup (120 ml) almond milk or milk of choice

Combine all the ingredients in a blender and blend for 1 minute, or until the butter melts.

OPTIONAL SUPER BOOSTS:

VANILLA, CHOCOLATE, OR PLAIN PROTEIN POWDER

REISHI

ASHWAGANDHA

PROBIOTIC POWDER

PINK HIMALAYAN SALT

I frequently appear as a judge on the Food Network show *Guy's Grocery Games*. It was behind the scenes on that show that I first encountered Bulletproof coffee, coffee blended with MCT oil and butter or ghee. Originally created as a drink for people living a ketogenic lifestyle, it is believed to have a massive positive impact on both energy and cognitive function as well as boosting your metabolism. Several of the crew members on *GGG* are way into it, and their fervor piqued my curiosity. At first, I was dubious about putting butter in my coffee, but that all changed after my first sip. The flavor is addictive and the texture is super creamy, so much so I was inspired to translate it into a smoothie. If you're a purist, substitute more coffee for the almond milk for an added jolt. However, the added almond milk does enhance the creaminess, so take your pick. To sweeten it, add one pitted date or 1 tablespoon honey, maple syrup, agave, or another sweetener.

Chocolate Avocado

Serves 1

Ingredients:

½ ripe avocado, pitted and peeled

½ cup (62 g) chopped zucchini

1 serving chocolate protein powder*

1 dried date, pitted

1 pinch pink Himalayan salt

¾ cup (180 ml) milk of choice

Handful of ice (optional, if you want it frostier!)

Combine all the ingredients in a blender and blend until smooth.

For a deeper chocolate flavor, replace the chocolate protein powder with 2 teaspoons cacao powder.

OPTIONAL SUPER BOOSTS:

BEE POLLEN

CHIA SEEDS

HEMP SEEDS

COLLAGEN PEPTIDES

REISHI

ASHWAGANDHA

PROBIOTIC POWDER

This recipe was a complete accident. It was one of those days I was surprised to discover I was out of almost all of my smoothie ingredient staples. All I turned up was a sample packet of chocolate protein powder and a lone zucchini from my vegetable garden. It felt like a random combination, to be sure, but my hangry set in, so into the blender they went. Well, I can't begin to tell you how spectacular that combo turned out to be. I refined the recipe, adding avocado for creaminess and a date for a touch of sweetness to bring out the chocolate. The resulting flavor is sumptuous.

Chocolate Nut

Serves 1

Ingredients:

1 frozen banana, peeled

1 tablespoon peanut or other nut butter

1 tablespoon cacao powder

¼ teaspoon vanilla extract or ⅛ teaspoon vanilla paste

½ cup (120 ml) milk of choice or water

1 dried date, pitted

2 ice cubes

Combine all the ingredients in a blender and blend until smooth.

OPTIONAL SUPER BOOSTS:

BEE POLLEN

CHIA SEEDS

FLAX SEEDS

VANILLA OR PLAIN PROTEIN POWDER

SPIRULINA

CHLORELLA

REISHI

ASHWAGANDHA

PROBIOTIC POWDER

GREENS POWDER

GOJI BERRIES

MACA POWDER

PINK HIMALAYAN SALT

BRAZIL NUTS

No exaggeration, every morning when I go in to wake up my youngest, the first word out of her mouth is smoothie. She's been drinking one every morning since she was less than a year old, and almost three years later it's her definition of breakfast. One of her most requested is this chocolate nut smoothie. I usually make it with peanut butter, as the taste evokes the healthiest Reese's Peanut Butter Cup you've ever had, but you can substitute sunflower butter or another nut butter.

Cacao Banana Date

Serves 1

Ingredients:

1 fresh or frozen banana, peeled

2 teaspoons cacao powder

2 dried dates, pitted

2 tablespoons almond butter

1 tablespoon flax seeds or flaxseed meal

1 cup (240 ml) milk of choice or water

Combine all the ingredients in a blender and blend until smooth.

OPTIONAL SUPER BOOSTS:

BEE POLLEN

CHIA SEEDS

HEMP SEEDS

VANILLA OR PLAIN PROTEIN POWDER

COLLAGEN PEPTIDES

REISHI

ASHWAGANDHA

PROBIOTIC POWDER

MACA POWDER

PINK HIMALAYAN SALT

BRAZIL NUTS

One of the best things about smoothies is that you can tailor them to suit whatever you're craving on any given day. I also like to create flavor mash-ups (pun intended). I'm a total chocolate and banana lover, and I pull off the road in a heartbeat whenever I see a sign for date shakes (they're a common sight on interstates in southern California), so I merged them all into this smoothie. Nutrient-rich cacao powder and the natural sweetness of vitamin-packed dates provide the chocolaty flavor you might have only thought possible from a sugary syrup. You don't have to twist my arm to drink a smoothie this good for you. For extra vegetable goodness, add ¼ cup (33 g) frozen cauliflower florets, fresh spinach, or zucchini. You won't detect the taste at all!

Chocolate Cherry

Serves 1

Ingredients:

¾ cup (116 g) fresh or frozen cherries, pitted

½ fresh or frozen banana, peeled

½ cup (15 g) fresh spinach

1 tablespoon cacao powder

1 serving collagen peptides

¾ cup (180 ml) milk of choice

Combine all the ingredients in a blender and blend until smooth.

OPTIONAL SUPER BOOSTS:

BEE POLLEN

CHIA SEEDS

HEMP SEEDS

FLAX SEEDS

VANILLA OR PLAIN PROTEIN POWDER

REISHI

ASHWAGANDHA

PROBIOTIC POWDER

MACA POWDER

PINK HIMALAYAN SALT

BRAZIL NUTS

There are certain foods I dream about all year long. Fresh cherries are at the top of that list. There's absolutely nothing like them, so whenever you can get your hands on a pint, I highly recommend you grab it. Luckily, frozen cherries can be just as delicious and, on occasion, even more so. Cherries are a potent source of antioxidants, and they are rich in potassium (almost as much as a banana), making this a great smoothie for anyone who works out and needs to soothe their aching muscles. What's more, ¾ cup (116 g) of cherries contains less than 75 calories. They're super sweet, so I keep this smoothie really simple, adding collagen to get a bang of protein and a spoonful of cacao powder for that classic, deep chocolate cherry flavor that's so hard to resist.

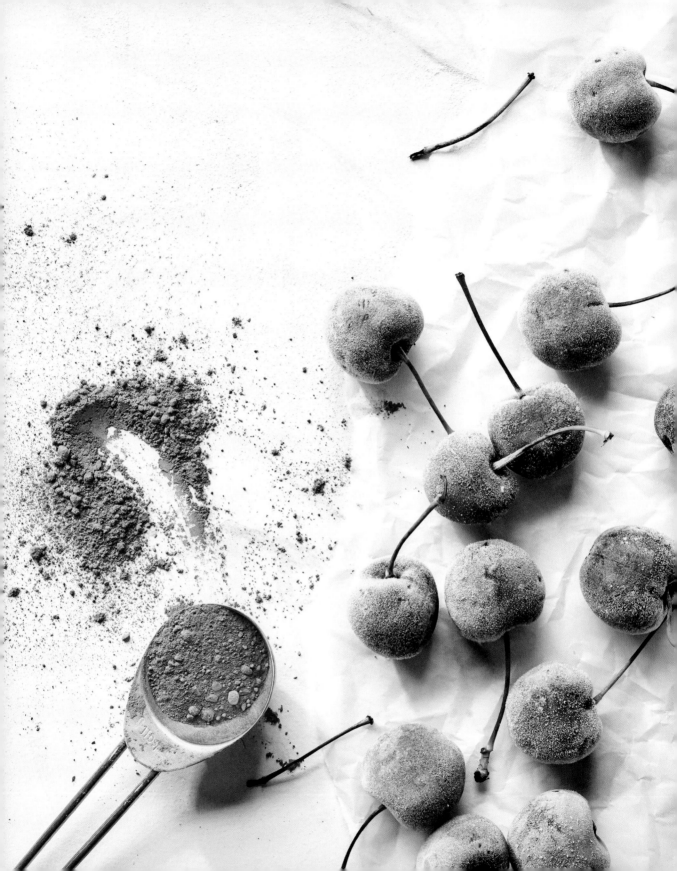

Creamy Vanilla Shake

Serves 1

Ingredients:

½ frozen banana, peeled

½ cup (66 g) frozen cauliflower florets

2 tablespoons cashews raw, unsalted or
1 tablespoon cashew butter*

1 serving collagen peptides

¼ teaspoon vanilla extract or ⅛ teaspoon
vanilla paste

2 dried dates, pitted

1 tablespoon hemp seeds

¾ cup (180 ml) almond milk or milk of choice

OPTIONAL SUPER BOOSTS:

BEE POLLEN

CHIA SEEDS

REISHI

ASHWAGANDHA

PROBIOTIC POWDER

MACA POWDER

PINK HIMALAYAN SALT

BRAZIL NUTS

**Combine all the ingredients in a blender
and blend until smooth.**

*If you don't have a high-powered blender, soak the
cashews overnight (discard the water before using) to
make them easier to puree perfectly smooth (see page
249). One serving of vanilla protein powder can be used
in place of the cashews or cashew butter.*

What's more all-American than a vanilla milkshake? I have countless childhood memories of sucking them down at Dairy Queen, but thinking about the ingredients they were made with gives me a chill. However, instead of ignoring my cravings, I prefer to find a way to create healthier versions to satisfy them.

This recipe takes creamy to a whole new level, hitting all the notes of the beloved vanilla milkshake of my youth, only it's entirely made up of real foods like dates, banana, cashews, vanilla, hemp seeds, even frozen cauliflower. It's the best "eat this, not that" shake you can imagine.

Matcha Date Shake

Serves 1

Ingredients:

1 frozen banana, peeled

1 teaspoon matcha green tea powder

¾ cup (22 g) fresh spinach

1 dried date, pitted

¼ teaspoon vanilla extract or ⅛ teaspoon vanilla paste

1 cup (240 ml) almond milk or milk of choice

1 cup ice

Combine all the ingredients in a blender and blend until smooth.

OPTIONAL SUPER BOOSTS:

BEE POLLEN

CHIA SEEDS

HEMP SEEDS

FLAX SEEDS

MACA POWDER

VANILLA OR PLAIN PROTEIN POWDER

COLLAGEN PEPTIDES

SPIRULINA

CHLORELLA

REISHI

ASHWAGANDHA

PROBIOTIC POWDER

PINK HIMALAYAN SALT

BRAZIL NUTS

Matcha, a prized Japanese green tea known for its powerful antioxidant properties, has become super trendy. Matcha lattes, ice cream, frozen yogurt, baked goods, milkshakes—it's become a major thing. Funny, since matcha has been around for thousands of years. This is my smoothie twist on a classic matcha latte with banana and spinach added for extra nourishment. Its intense emerald green color will please your eyes as much as your tummy.

Matcha is packed with antioxidants.

Mocha Almond

Serves 1

Ingredients:

1 cup (240 ml) cold brew coffee or your favorite strong-brewed coffee

1 frozen banana, peeled

1 tablespoon cacao powder

1 tablespoon almond butter

1 serving collagen peptides

2 teaspoons coconut oil

1 pinch pink Himalayan salt

2 tablespoons milk of choice

3 ice cubes

Combine all the ingredients in a blender and blend until smooth.

OPTIONAL SUPER BOOSTS:

BEE POLLEN

CHIA SEEDS

HEMP SEEDS

FLAX SEEDS

MACA POWDER

VANILLA OR PLAIN PROTEIN POWDER

MCT OIL

REISHI

ASHWAGANDHA

PROBIOTIC POWDER

BRAZIL NUTS

I have to have coffee in the morning. Which may strike you as unusual when you find out that I only drink decaf. My default mode is Energizer Bunny (much to my husband's annoyance), and caffeine makes me jumpy. However, I love a daily cup to get my day going—simply the smell of it makes me happy.

If you love your morning coffee and think you have to choose between that or a smoothie to start your day, this smoothie will blow your mind. Packed with protein from the almond butter and collagen peptides in a base of cold brew, it will keep you fully charged and sated but also light on your toes till lunch.

berry heavy

Blueberry Magic Lemonade

Serves 1

Ingredients:

1 cup (148 g) frozen blueberries

½ lemon (with peel and pith), seeds removed

¼ cup (60 ml) plain or vanilla yogurt

1 serving Blue Majik

1 tablespoon honey

⅛ teaspoon ground cardamom

½ cup (120 ml) coconut water

Combine all the ingredients in a blender and blend until smooth.

OPTIONAL SUPER BOOSTS:

BEE POLLEN

CHIA SEEDS

HEMP SEEDS

FLAX SEEDS

VANILLA OR PLAIN PROTEIN POWDER

COLLAGEN PEPTIDES

MCT OIL

REISHI

ASHWAGANDHA

PROBIOTIC POWDER

GREENS POWDER

CAMU CAMU POWDER

MACA POWDER

BRAZIL NUTS

While it may not seem like an obvious flavor combination, I find that there are few things more refreshing in summertime than a tall, cold glass of lemonade alongside a bowl of fresh blueberries. What if you could have the best of both all in one glass with a little bit of magic—literally—sprinkled in for good measure? You can. Blue Majik is the product name of a spirulina algae extract sold by the company E3Live. While one of its coolest properties is its brilliant blue color and the ability to produce some eye-poppingly cool shades of azure smoothies and "nice" creams, it claims to have serious antioxidant properties, along with other health benefits like inflammation support. Combined with the protein and digestive enzymes in the yogurt and the hydrating coconut water, this light smoothie is a great one to drink after you exercise. It will give you anything but the blues!

Açaí "Bowl"

Ingredients:

½ pack (1.75 ounces/50 g) frozen açaí

½ fresh or frozen banana, peeled

½ cup (74 g) mixed frozen berries (raspberries, blueberries, blackberries, and/or strawberries)

1 fresh kale leaf, thick stem removed, chopped

1 tablespoon hemp seeds

1 tablespoon chia seeds

¾ cup (180 ml) almond milk or milk of choice

Toppings (optional): fresh berries, bee pollen, shaved coconut, and/or granola

Combine all the ingredients in a blender and blend until smooth. Pour the smoothie into a serving glass and add your choice of toppings.

OPTIONAL SUPER BOOSTS:

BEE POLLEN

COLLAGEN PEPTIDES

REISHI

ASHWAGANDHA

GOLDEN BERRIES

Over the past few years I've become hooked on açaí bowls. Açaí is a deep purple South American superfood berry that's packed with antioxidant properties, calcium, fiber, and vitamin A. Blended frozen and topped with a variety of healthful toppings, they're a frozen treat with understandable popularity—shops selling them seem to have popped up everywhere. Not only are açaí bowls, with their deep berry taste, addictive, but another fun way to simultaneously get in many of your favorite boosts—like granola, shaved coconut, chia seeds, bee pollen, and more. While I love eating a bowl, turning it into a smoothie, combined with potassium-rich bananas and plenty of protein, makes it easy to take a favorite on the go.

Berry Vanilla Shake

Serves 1

Ingredients:

½ cup (75 g) frozen strawberries

½ cup (65 g) frozen raspberries

¼ cup (33 g) frozen cauliflower florets

1 serving vanilla protein powder

½ cup (120 ml) vanilla Greek or regular yogurt

¾ cup (180 ml) milk of choice

Combine all the ingredients in a blender and blend until smooth.

OPTIONAL SUPER BOOSTS:

BEE POLLEN

CHIA SEEDS

HEMP SEEDS

FLAX SEEDS

MACA POWDER

COLLAGEN PEPTIDES

MCT OIL

GOJI BERRIES

BRAZIL NUTS

While not as scientific a description as, say, the difference between a crocodile and an alligator, there is a fine line between a smoothie and a milkshake. We generally think of milkshakes as decadent, rich, and creamy, made with a base of milk and ice cream, the latter of which you will obviously never find in a smoothie!

But what if you could recreate the decadence of a milkshake in the form of a healthy smoothie? This smoothie does just that, with tons of protein from Greek yogurt, vanilla protein powder, and milk and fiber from berries. It's just as filling, satisfying, and colorful as the ice cream parlor classic, only its bright red color comes entirely from fruit with no refined sugars or fillers to weigh you down. Whether you decide to call this a smoothie or a shake matters not, because that naughty itch will be scratched in the best way possible.

Big Red

Serves 1

Ingredients:

½ cup (75 g) frozen strawberries

½ cup (65 g) frozen raspberries

¼ small raw or cooked beet, peeled and cut into 1-inch (2.5-cm) pieces

1 dried date, pitted

1 tablespoon goji berries

1 tablespoon chia seeds

¾ cup (180 ml) milk of choice

Combine all the ingredients in a blender and blend until smooth.

OPTIONAL SUPER BOOSTS:

BEE POLLEN

HEMP SEEDS

FLAX SEEDS

MACA POWDER

VANILLA OR PLAIN PROTEIN POWDER

COLLAGEN PEPTIDES

MCT OIL

PROBIOTIC POWDER

AÇAÍ POWDER

CAMU CAMU POWDER

PINK HIMALAYAN SALT

BRAZIL NUTS

The brighter the color of fruits and vegetables, the more nutrients they generally possess. This smoothie gets its bright red color from strawberries, raspberries, goji berries, and, yes, beets. Some people might be put off with the words *beet* and *smoothie* in the same sentence, but in this combination it's a taste to fall in love with—not to mention that beets are packed with fiber and nutrients that can boost energy, stamina, and vitality and repair the cell damage caused by inflammation. If you prefer an even beet-ier flavor, simply add more than the recipe calls for, but I find this amount to be spot-on.

Blue Chia

Serves 1

Ingredients:

¾ cup (111 g) frozen blueberries

½ fresh or frozen banana, peeled

2 teaspoons chia seeds

2 teaspoons hemp seeds

1 tablespoon almond or cashew butter

1 cup (240 ml) almond milk or milk of choice

Combine all the ingredients in a blender and blend until smooth.

OPTIONAL SUPER BOOSTS:

BEE POLLEN

VANILLA OR PLAIN PROTEIN POWDER

COLLAGEN PEPTIDES

MCT OIL

REISHI

ASHWAGANDHA

PROBIOTIC POWDER

There are two things I hate being when I leave the house in the morning: rushed and hungry. With three kids, a husband, a dog, and a full-time job, it can be a real struggle to get out the door most days. This smoothie has recently become one of my go-tos, as the ingredients are basic ones I always have on hand. It's packed with antioxidants from the blueberries and protein from the chia seeds, hemp seeds, and nut butter. It keeps you plenty full, but it's easy to digest. If you want to take it up a notch, toss in a few green cubes (see page 84) or a handful of fresh greens. Or just enjoy it just the way it is. You're rushed enough.

Blueberry Cherry Lemon

Serves 1

Ingredients:

¾ cup (111 g) frozen blueberries

¼ cup (38 g) frozen cherries, pitted

¼ lemon (with peel and pith), seeds removed

2 tablespoons coconut yogurt

⅛ teaspoon ground cardamom

1 tablespoon hemp seeds

1 tablespoon honey or blue agave

¾ cup (180 ml) almond milk or milk of choice

Combine all the ingredients in a blender and blend until smooth.

OPTIONAL SUPER BOOSTS:

BEE POLLEN

CHIA SEEDS

FLAX SEEDS

MACA POWDER

VANILLA OR PLAIN PROTEIN POWDER

COLLAGEN PEPTIDES

REISHI

ASHWAGANDHA

PROBIOTIC POWDER GOJI BERRIES

AÇAÍ POWDER

CAMU CAMU POWDER

MAQUI BERRY POWDER

PINK HIMALAYAN SALT

BRAZIL NUTS

Asking me to pick my favorite Smoothie Project recipe is like asking me to pick my favorite child. It's impossible; however, this recipe is way up there. Not only is it an antioxidant bomb, it's also totally habit-forming. The call for a quarter lemon including the skin is not a typo, so make sure to do it, as there's tons of nutrition and flavor in both the peel and flesh. The lemon also brings out all the subtleties of the cherries, which, aside from being delicious, contain anthocyanin, which is believed to reduce the effects of aging and improve memory function. I keep this smoothie vegan by using coconut yogurt because I prefer its zippy flavor profile in this recipe, but you can use plain or vanilla cow's milk or another plant-based yogurt if you prefer. I can't wait for you to try this smoothie!

Blueberry Coconut Goji

Serves 1

Ingredients:

½ fresh banana, peeled

½ cup (74 g) fresh or frozen blueberries

½ cup (50 g) frozen coconut sheets or chunks

¼ cup (8 g) fresh spinach

1 tablespoon goji berries

1 serving collagen peptides or vanilla protein powder

¾ cup (180 ml) coconut water

Combine all the ingredients in a blender and blend until smooth.

OPTIONAL SUPER BOOSTS:

BEE POLLEN

CHIA SEEDS

HEMP SEEDS

FLAX SEEDS

MACA POWDER

REISHI

ASHWAGANDHA

PROBIOTIC POWDER

PINK HIMALAYAN SALT

BRAZIL NUTS

One of my dearest friends is an acupuncturist and practitioner of Chinese medicine who is also into healing foods. One summer day many years ago, she came over with a bag of trail mix that was nothing like the packaged brands I was familiar with. This one was filled with cacao nibs, golden berries, nuts, seeds, and goji berries. This was also my first introduction to goji berries—a sweet, slightly sour, bright orangish-pink raisin-like fruit.

Eaten for centuries in China, goji berries are believed to boost your immunity, promote calmness, improve sleep, and even aid in weight loss. They're also lower in calories and sugar than other dried fruits. When you try this smoothie, you'll understand why they're always in my pantry.

Blueberr-Z

Ingredients:

¾ cup (111 g) frozen blueberries

½ fresh or frozen banana, peeled

¼ cup (31) fresh or frozen chopped zucchini

¼ cup (8 g) fresh spinach

1 tablespoon hemp seeds

⅛ teaspoon ground cinnamon

½ cup (120 ml) almond milk or milk of choice

Combine all the ingredients in a blender and blend until smooth.

OPTIONAL SUPER BOOSTS:

BEE POLLEN

CHIA SEEDS

HEMP SEEDS

FLAX SEEDS

MACA POWDER

VANILLA OR PLAIN PROTEIN POWDER

COLLAGEN PEPTIDES

REISHI

ASHWAGANDHA

PROBIOTIC POWDER

GOJI BERRIES

AÇAÍ POWDER

CAMU CAMU POWDER

MAQUI BERRY POWDER

PINK HIMALAYAN SALT

BRAZIL NUTS

Zucchini grows like a weed in my garden. When they're in season I sauté, steam, zoodle, and air-fry them but still have more remaining than we can eat. That's why I like to slice and freeze them raw to use year-round in smoothies. Zucchini may seem like an unusual ingredient to add to a smoothie, but it couldn't be more at home in your blender. Low in calories and high in anti-inflammatory properties, zucchini adds a lot of body to your smoothie with a mild, unobtrusive flavor that lets the blueberry and cinnamon become the stars of the show.

Pregnancy

Serves 1

Ingredients:

1 frozen banana, peeled

½ cup (65 g) frozen blackberries

1 (10-ounce/283-g) bag frozen raspberries

1 serving chocolate or vanilla protein powder

1 serving greens powder

1 serving collagen peptides

1 serving probiotic powder

2 teaspoons hemp seeds

1 teaspoon bee pollen

1 pinch pink Himalayan salt

Combine all the ingredients in a blender and blend until smooth.

During my first pregnancy, I believed I could eat everything under the sun, and trust me when I say I really went for it. However, I learned my lesson, and by my second pregnancy, I seriously pulled on the reins of restraint by focusing on a super healthy diet while still trying to find foods to satisfy my itch for chocolate. This smoothie became my everything.

Digestion can slow down when you're pregnant, so my midwife advised me to eat tons of raspberries, as they have more fiber cup-for-cup than other fruits. I doubled down by also adding blackberries to the smoothie. And as moms-to-be want to make sure they are receiving tons of nutrients to help baby grow, I added hemp seeds for those essential omega-3 fatty acids; greens powder for much-needed iron; probiotics; and a pinch of pink Himalayan salt for nutrient absorption.

I looked forward to this smoothie every morning, not just for how rich and chocolaty it was (it's equally nom nom with vanilla), but also because I knew that I was supporting my baby's growth with the best foods possible. It was my go-to for my entire pregnancy and straight through nursing to support milk production.

Strawberry "Nice" Cream

Serves 1

Ingredients:

1 cup (150 g) frozen strawberries

½ frozen banana, peeled

1 serving collagen peptides

2 tablespoons cashews raw, unsalted*
or 1 serving vanilla protein powder

2 tablespoons to ⅓ cup (70 ml) milk of
choice, depending on desired thickness

OPTIONAL SUPER BOOSTS:

BEE POLLEN

HEMP SEEDS

FLAX SEEDS

MACA POWDER

MCT OIL

REISHI

ASHWAGANDHA

Combine the strawberries, banana, collagen peptides, and cashews in a high-powered blender with a plunger tamper attachment and start by adding 2 tablespoons milk.

Turn the blender to high and use the tamper to push down the ingredients until they just start coming together. Use more milk, 1 tablespoon at a time, as needed until it turns into ice cream.

If your blender doesn't have a tamper, stop the blender periodically and push down the ingredients with a wooden spoon. To make the texture even more ice cream like, place the "nice" cream in a bowl or cup and freeze for 30 minutes to 1 hour.

My first "nice" cream experience was twelve years ago at the house of a friend who also happens to be a vegan with a sweet tooth. At the time, there weren't many choices for vegan ice cream, and most options tasted chalky at best. The closest thing to ice cream she created was frozen bananas that she ran through a Yonanas machine. When I got home and tried the same basic recipe in my blender, I realized I could achieve the same effect, and even experimented adding other frozen fruits. The combo that stood out for me was this take on strawberry ice cream. The low-in-sugar strawberries also add an extra boost of vitamin C. To give it protein, I add collagen peptides and protein powder, but opt for the cashews if you want to keep it vegan. This is the kind of sweet treat you can eat any time of day and feel good about yourself, bite after bite.

Strawberry Coconut

Serves 1

Ingredients:

1 cup (150 g) fresh or frozen strawberries

¼ cup (25 g) frozen coconut sheets or chunks

¼ cup (33 g) frozen cauliflower florets

1 serving vanilla protein powder

¾ cup (180 ml) almond milk

Combine all the ingredients in a blender and blend until smooth.

OPTIONAL SUPER BOOSTS:

BEE POLLEN

HEMP SEEDS

CHIA SEEDS

COLLAGEN PEPTIDES

REISHI

ASHWAGANDHA

FRESH MINT

When I create a recipe for the Smoothie Project, I test it at least several times, perfecting it along the way. On the other hand, my husband tends to put a different spin on the same type of smoothie every day, leaving me and our kids to be the taste testers. His smoothies are packed with so many fruits, vegetables, dark leafy greens, and superfoods that they almost always have an intense dark color, so one morning when I saw this pink smoothie in his hand I was totally taken aback.

He told me he wanted to see how the combination of strawberry and coconut would taste. Clearly pretty good, considering how often he made it after that. Although it contains only five ingredients, they come together with vibrant flavor and a brilliant, lush texture. The frozen cauliflower keeps the smoothie leaner and gets a veggie in, which I love. And if you're not used to buying frozen coconut, it's time to start. It's a sweet and creamy smoothie ingredient that also adds incredible flavor and texture to "nice" creams. I like to use frozen sheets or chunks. They're easy to measure and add into smoothies.

Pink Milk

Serves 1

Ingredients:

¾ cup (112 g) fresh or frozen strawberries

1 cup (240 ml) milk of choice

1 tablespoon honey

Combine all the ingredients in a blender and blend until smooth.

OPTIONAL SUPER BOOSTS:

BEE POLLEN

CHIA SEEDS

HEMP SEEDS

MACA POWDER

FLAX SEEDS

VANILLA OR PLAIN PROTEIN POWDER

COLLAGEN PEPTIDES

PROBIOTIC POWDER

GOJI BERRIES

PINK HIMALAYAN SALT

BRAZIL NUTS

Did you ever drink strawberry milk when you were a kid? While I was more of a plain or chocolate milk kid, many of my friends loved it. It had a bright, fake-pink color and was so über-sugary sweet to me that I couldn't get it down.

All those negative associations vanish with this smoothie. It's the dreamiest version of the strawberry milk you drank as a kid, only a hundred times better (and healthier). You can make it with frozen strawberries any time of year, or try it with juicy, fresh strawberries when you can get your hands on them in summertime. It's a perfect wholesome treat for big and little kids alike.

clean + clear

Berry Green

Serves 1

Ingredients:

1 cup (30 g) fresh spinach

1 orange, peeled and seeded

½ cup (75 g) frozen strawberries

1 tablespoon chia seeds

½ cup (120 ml) coconut water

1 handful ice

Combine all the ingredients in a blender and blend until smooth.

OPTIONAL SUPER BOOSTS:

BEE POLLEN

HEMP SEEDS

FLAX SEEDS

MACA POWDER

VANILLA OR PLAIN PROTEIN POWDER

COLLAGEN PEPTIDES

MCT OIL

SPIRULINA

CHLORELLA

REISHI

ASHWAGANDHA

PROBIOTIC POWDER

I probably shouldn't admit to how I came up with this smoothie, but it's a great example of what you can do with whatever basic smoothie ingredients are in your fridge and pantry on any given day. Our family had been traveling for a week, and I was rustling about trying to figure out what I could make with the little that was there when I discovered an orange with skin so dehydrated I could barely peel it (oranges in this condition can still be juicy—if not at their nutritional peak), some fiber-rich frozen strawberries, and a bag of farmers' market spinach that miraculously was not wilted (greens have a long fridge life if you store them properly—see page 34). I grabbed a coconut water from the pantry (always handy for smoothie emergencies) and some chia seeds, tossed everything in the blender, and this baby was created. It's an incredibly nourishing, vitamin C–packed smoothie that quenches your thirst while leaving you feeling lean and mean.

Apple Beet Ginger

Serves 1

Ingredients:

1 Gala, Fuji, or other sweet apple, cored, seeded, and cut into chunks*

¼ raw or cooked beet, peeled and cut into 1-inch (2.5-cm) pieces

1 small carrot, peeled and chopped (about ¼ cup/32 g)

½ cup (15 g) fresh spinach

½-inch (1.25-cm) piece fresh ginger, peeled

2 teaspoons fresh lemon juice

1 serving collagen peptides

¾ cup (180 ml) coconut water

1 handful ice

Combine all the ingredients in a blender and blend until smooth.

If you don't have a high-powered blender, peel the apple.

OPTIONAL SUPER BOOSTS:

BEE POLLEN

HEMP SEEDS

CHIA SEEDS

REISHI

ASHWAGANDHA

FRESH MINT

Twenty years ago I made my first of several trips to a detox spa in the California desert that prescribed periods of fasting, determined to put an end to my excessive sugar cravings. I was convinced I wouldn't last the four days, but by the end of the trip I had majorly curbed that sweet tooth. Once every day, we got to enjoy a small glass of fresh-pressed apple, beet, and ginger juice. When you're not eating, even the tiniest bit of nourishment tastes incredible, and I still dream about the flavors of that juice.

Inspired by that magical juice, this smoothie has the perfectly balanced, fresh tastes of sweet apple, bright lemon, and warm ginger bursting through in every sip. I add spinach to get my greens and collagen peptides for protein. If you love the consistency of juice but still want the fiber of a smoothie, this drink is for you.

Carrot Orange Ginger

Serves 1

Ingredients:

½ fresh or frozen banana, peeled

1 orange, peeled and seeded

1 small carrot, peeled and chopped (about ¼ cup/32 g)

½-inch (1.25-cm) piece fresh ginger, peeled

½ cup (120 ml) coconut water

Combine all the ingredients in a blender and blend until smooth.

OPTIONAL SUPER BOOSTS:

BEE POLLEN

CHIA SEEDS

HEMP SEEDS

FLAX SEEDS

MACA POWDER

VANILLA OR PLAIN PROTEIN POWDER

COLLAGEN PEPTIDES

MCT OIL

PROBIOTIC POWDER

FRESH OR GROUND TURMERIC

A few years ago, after experiencing sticker shock from the immunity-boosting shots I bought for my family in the health food store, I started making my own. When you're sick, fresh ginger is high on the list of healing foods that you should be adding to your diet. Ginger is also effective at reducing nausea and motion sickness and decreasing inflammation. Carrots are high in the powerful infection fighter vitamin A and beta-carotene, which reinforces the mucus membranes that line the respiratory and intestinal tracts, making it more difficult for bacteria to enter the bloodstream. Potassium-packed banana, vitamin C–rich orange, and hydrating coconut water round out the party, for a smoothie that's perfect to enjoy throughout the winter to keep your immune system strong and your taste buds satisfied.

Replenish

Serves 1

Ingredients:

½ fresh or frozen banana, peeled

2 fresh kale leaves, thick stems removed, chopped

1 dried date, pitted

4 raw walnut halves

½ cup (120 ml) coconut milk

½ cup (120 ml) coconut water

Combine all the ingredients in a blender and blend until smooth.

OPTIONAL SUPER BOOSTS:

BEE POLLEN

CHIA SEEDS

HEMP SEEDS

FLAX SEEDS

MACA POWDER

VANILLA OR PLAIN PROTEIN POWDER

COLLAGEN PEPTIDES

MCT OIL

REISHI

ASHWAGANDHA

PROBIOTIC POWDER

GOJI BERRIES

AÇAÍ POWDER

CAMU CAMU POWDER

MAQUI BERRY POWDER

PINK HIMALAYAN SALT

BRAZIL NUTS

Sports drinks like Gatorade are intended to hydrate and replenish the electrolytes lost during physical activity, but it comes at a cost when you consider the dangerous food dyes and sugar that come along with them. This smoothie is made with natural coconut water, which contains key electrolytes like calcium, magnesium, and phosphorus, and is packed with other nutrients like potassium (more than is found in one banana or fifteen sport drinks) and sodium. Blend it up with kale, banana, a date for sweetness, and walnuts for protein, and you've got a fiber-filled post-exercise smoothie with a dazzling green color that will leave you hydrated and restored.

Detox

Serves 1

Ingredients:

½ fresh or frozen banana, peeled

½ cup (80 g) fresh or frozen pineapple chunks

½ Gala, Fuji, or other sweet apple, cored, seeded, and cut into chunks*

1 cup (30 g) fresh spinach

¾ cup (180 ml) water or coconut water

Combine all the ingredients in a blender and blend until smooth.

*If you don't have a high-powered blender, peel the apple.

OPTIONAL SUPER BOOSTS:

BEE POLLEN

CHIA SEEDS

HEMP SEEDS

FLAX SEEDS

MACA POWDER

VANILLA OR PLAIN PROTEIN POWDER

COLLAGEN PEPTIDES

MCT OIL

SPIRULINA

CHLORELLA

REISHI

ASHWAGANDHA

PROBIOTIC POWDER

When your body's natural detoxification system slows down due to poor diet, stress, an autoimmune condition, or other ailment, it may be time to allow your body to detox, to replace a heavy meal with a clean, light smoothie like this one. There are only fruits and vegetables in this smoothie, making it very cleansing. Whenever I can get my hands on a fresh, super sweet pineapple, I grab it. Pineapple is a powerful fruit with considerable benefits. It's easy to digest and also reduces inflammation, making it particularly helpful with swelling that occurs in conditions like sinusitis, sore throats, and colds.

Light and Bright

Serves 1

Ingredients:

1 thick slice raw beet, peeled (about 2 tablespoons)

¼ lemon (with peel and pith), seeds removed

½ Gala, Fuji, or other sweet apple, cored, seeded, and cut into chunks*

1 small carrot, peeled and chopped (about ¼ cup/32 g)

1 tablespoon goji berries

1 pinch pink Himalayan salt

¾ cup (180 ml) coconut water

Combine all the ingredients in a blender and blend until smooth.

If you don't have a high-powered blender, peel the apple.

OPTIONAL SUPER BOOSTS:

BEE POLLEN

CHIA SEEDS

HEMP SEEDS

FLAX SEEDS

MACA POWDER

VANILLA OR PLAIN PROTEIN POWDER

COLLAGEN PEPTIDES

MCT OIL

REISHI

ASHWAGANDHA

PROBIOTIC POWDER

One of the bonuses of living in Los Angeles is that when you're in need of a nutritious smoothie in a hurry, there is an abundance of smoothie shops located throughout the city. I got the idea for this smoothie from one of my favorites, Kreation Juice. This smoothie includes beets, which help to purify your blood and liver; vitamin A–packed carrots to promote immunity function and improve eye health; and lemon to fight fatigue. Apple helps satisfy hunger pangs, while coconut water provides valuable electrolytes.

Crazy Healthy

Serves 1

Ingredients:

½ fresh or frozen banana, peeled

1 small carrot, peeled and chopped
(about ¼ cup/32 g)

¼ beet, peeled

2 fresh kale leaves, thick stems
removed, chopped

1 cup frozen fruit (anything you love)

1 dried date, pitted

1 teaspoon hemp seeds

1 teaspoon chia seeds

1 teaspoon bee pollen

4 raw walnut halves

¾ cup (180 ml) milk of choice, coconut water,
or water

**Combine all the ingredients in a blender
and blend until smooth.**

OPTIONAL SUPER BOOSTS:

COLLAGEN PEPTIDES

PROTEIN POWDER

FLAX SEEDS

REISHI

ASHWAGANDHA

GOLDEN BERRIES

My sweet husband went through a period where he was burning the candle at both ends. He was traveling nonstop and working sixteen-hour days, six to seven days a week. He wasn't sleeping or getting any exercise and felt totally rundown. Each morning, however, he would get out of bed, after just a few hours of sleep, to take the kids to school and pull out an outrageous amount of nutrient-dense ingredients in order to make what I've always called his Crazy Healthy Smoothie. I had never seen so many ingredients shoved into a blender, but as he left the house every day for another absurdly long day of work, I knew that smoothie was more than just a meal for him. It was the one thing that kept him feeling nourished and happy. This is a slightly pared-down version, but if you want to make it closer to his original, add the super boosts and as many other fruits and vegetables as you like. This is truly health in a massive glass.

Carrot Apple Mango

Serves 1

Ingredients:

¾ cup (120 g) frozen mango chunks

½ Gala, Fuji, or other sweet apple, cored, seeded, and cut into chunks*

1 small carrot, peeled (about ¼ cup/32 g)

2 tablespoons cashews raw, unsalted

¾ cup (180 ml) milk of choice

Combine all the ingredients in a blender and blend until smooth.

If you don't have a high-powered blender, peel the apple.

OPTIONAL SUPER BOOSTS:

BEE POLLEN

CHIA SEEDS

HEMP SEEDS

FLAX SEEDS

VANILLA OR PLAIN PROTEIN POWDER

COLLAGEN PEPTIDES

MCT OIL

REISHI

ASHWAGANDHA

PROBIOTIC POWDER

GOJI BERRIES

CAMU CAMU POWDER

MACA POWDER

BRAZIL NUTS

GOLDEN BERRIES

My son will drink just about any smoothie I put in front of him. It's kind of amazing to watch him suck down an entire 10-ounce glass every morning no matter what flavor it is. The one thing I've learned about his favorite combos, though, is that he prefers fruit-forward smoothies; the fewer ingredients the better, like this smoothie. Its vibrant salmon color comes from mango and carrot, ingredients that pack a lot of flavor as well as vitamin A, C, and beta-carotene. In spite of how light it is, it will keep you full for hours to come. Simple never tasted so good.

Simple never tasted so good

decadent

You're Nuts!

Ingredients:

1 fresh or frozen banana, peeled

¼ cup (33 g) frozen cauliflower florets

1 tablespoon almond butter

1 tablespoon peanut butter*

2 Brazil nuts**

¼ teaspoon ground cinnamon

1 cup (240 ml) almond milk or milk of choice

2 ice cubes

Combine all the ingredients in a blender and blend until smooth.

*If you have a peanut allergy, you can substitute any of your favorite nut or seed butters for peanut butter.

**If you don't have a high-powered blender, soak Brazil nuts for 1 hour to overnight.

OPTIONAL SUPER BOOSTS:

BEE POLLEN

HEMP SEEDS

CHIA SEEDS

COLLAGEN PEPTIDES

REISHI

ASHWAGANDHA

Whenever I'm super hungry and want to feel sated for hours, I make this nutty smoothie. With just the right amount of natural sweetness, a dash of cinnamon, and almond milk for creaminess, it will make you nuts for nuts!

Nut butters stay fresh in the refrigerator for months, and whole nuts can be frozen for up to one to two years, making them the perfect protein and healthy fat addition to have on hand at all times. You certainly could make this smoothie with just one type of nut or nut butter, but three—peanut, almonds, and Brazil nuts—are better than one. Brazil nuts are a great source of selenium, which can be challenging for vegetarians to get. Just one nut gives you the recommended daily allowance.

Banana Split

Serves 1

Ingredients:

1 frozen banana, peeled

1 tablespoon almond or peanut butter

1 tablespoon cacao powder

¼ teaspoon vanilla extract or ⅛ teaspoon vanilla paste

½ cup (120 ml) milk of choice

1 dried date, pitted

Toppings (optional): fresh or frozen cherries, slices of fresh banana, strawberries, grated coconut, cacao nibs, chocolate drizzle, and/or coconut whipped cream

Combine all the ingredients in a blender and blend until smooth. Pour into a serving glass lined with slices of fresh banana, if using, and then add any of the other toppings that you want to use.

OPTIONAL SUPER BOOSTS:

BEE POLLEN

CHIA SEEDS

HEMP SEEDS

FLAX SEEDS

MACA POWDER

VANILLA OR PLAIN PROTEIN POWDER

COLLAGEN PEPTIDES

PINK HIMALAYAN SALT

My mother didn't allow my brother and me many sweets when we were kids, which only made me want them more. I was notorious for getting my hands on kids' vitamins and popping them like they were Tic Tacs, which I wasn't allowed to have either. Once every few weeks my dad would shuffle us into the car and take us to Baskin-Robbins for a treat. I'd generally get a scoop or two, but on extra-special occasions he'd let me get one of my favorite desserts: a classic banana split. Eating it was a kind of religious experience. I was meticulous about it. Every bite had to be perfect, with a little ice cream, banana, nut, and strawberry in each spoonful.

I still love me a banana split every now and then, but, you know, I'm not a kid anymore. That's why I developed this smoothie that you can eat with a spoon. And if you want to take it to a whole other level, add any or all of the toppings for the ultimate healthful indulgence.

Chocolate Berry "Nice" Cream

Serves 1

Ingredients:

½ cup (65 g) frozen raspberries

½ cup (65 g) frozen blackberries

½ frozen banana, peeled

1 serving chocolate protein powder*

1 serving collagen peptides

⅓ cup (70 ml) milk of choice

Combine all the ingredients in a blender. Blend on a medium speed, using the tamper to push down the ingredients into the blades until the mixture is just pureed, making sure not to overblend.**

For a deeper chocolate flavor, replace the chocolate protein powder with 2 teaspoons cacao powder. Add one pitted date if you'd like extra sweetness.

***If your blender doesn't have a tamper, stop the blender periodically and push down the ingredients with a wooden spoon. To make the texture even more ice cream like, place the "nice" cream in a bowl or cup and freeze for 30 minutes to 1 hour.*

OPTIONAL SUPER BOOSTS:

BEE POLLEN

CHIA SEEDS

HEMP SEEDS

FLAX SEEDS

MACA POWDER

PROBIOTIC POWDER

GREENS POWDER

PINK HIMALAYAN SALT

As mentioned earlier, one of my greatest blender achievements was making "nice" cream, a totally healthy version of everyone's favorite frozen confection.

The tastiest versions of this treat begin with plenty of bananas, which form the sweet and creamy base. But you can lighten it further by replacing some of the banana with other fruits, such as fiber- and antioxidant-rich frozen berries. I use chocolate protein powder for this recipe, but you can easily replace it with cacao powder for a deeper chocolate flavor. Collagen peptides enhance the silkiness of this "nice" cream (as well as the health of your hair and nails). Experiment with some super boosts for added texture and nutrients in every lick.

Mint Chocolate

Serves 1

Ingredients:

1 frozen banana, peeled

½ cup (15 g) fresh spinach

5 fresh mint leaves

1 tablespoon cacao nibs

1 tablespoon cashew butter

½ teaspoon chlorella

1 serving collagen peptides

¾ cup (180 ml) milk of choice

Combine all the ingredients in a blender and blend until smooth.

OPTIONAL SUPER BOOSTS:

BEE POLLEN

CHIA SEEDS

HEMP SEEDS

Chocolate and mint make one of the greatest food marriages ever. There's something about the combination of the deep, earthy-sweet flavor of chocolate and the cool, light, brightness of mint that make my taste buds celebrate. If you've never tried this pairing in a smoothie, now is the perfect time to start. I add a handful of fresh spinach (you can swap it out for a few green cubes, page 84, if desired) for iron; chlorella, a freshwater algae packed with protein and vitamin B12; cashew butter and collagen for protein; and banana to sweeten it naturally. For all of you chocolate-mint ice cream lovers out there, meet its healthier and equally delicious cousin.

Cookies 'n' Cream

Serves 1

Ingredients:

½ fresh or frozen banana, peeled

¼ cup (33 g) frozen cauliflower florets

¼ cup (60 ml) vanilla yogurt

1 tablespoon cacao powder

1 tablespoon cacao nibs

¼ teaspoon vanilla extract or ⅛ teaspoon vanilla paste

1 cup (240 ml) milk of choice

Combine all the ingredients in a blender and blend until smooth.

OPTIONAL SUPER BOOSTS:

BEE POLLEN

HEMP SEEDS

CHIA SEEDS

VANILLA PROTEIN POWDER

COLLAGEN PEPTIDES

Cookies 'n' cream is one of my favorite ice cream flavors, but don't worry (or be disappointed), this recipe doesn't call for cookies. Instead, I add plenty of cacao, both powder and nibs, to give it that deep chocolaty cookie flavor and texture, and vanilla yogurt, vanilla extract, frozen cauliflower, and milk to re-create all the creamy attributes of ice cream. To sweeten it more, you can add a pitted date.

Cotton Candy

Serves 1

Ingredients:

1 cup (150 g) frozen strawberries

¼ cup (33 g) frozen cauliflower florets

¾ cup (180 ml) milk of choice

¼ cup (60 ml) plain or vanilla yogurt

1 tablespoon honey

Toppings (optional): fresh strawberries, frozen raspberries, frozen blackberries, frozen blueberries, honeycomb, honey, bee pollen, and/or granola

Combine all the ingredients in a blender and blend until smooth. Pour the smoothie into a serving glass and add your toppings of choice.

OPTIONAL SUPER BOOSTS:

BEE POLLEN

HEMP SEEDS

CHIA SEEDS

COLLAGEN PEPTIDES

VANILLA PROTEIN POWDER

A few years ago I did a collaboration with Black Tap restaurant in New York City. They're famous for their towering "crazy shakes," topped with everything from crumbled cookies to gooey syrups, which taste as outrageously delicious as they look. When they asked me to make a healthy version of their strawberry-flavored cotton candy milkshake, which is topped with rock candy, cotton candy, whipped cream, and a lollipop, I really had my work cut out for me.

Replicating the strawberry flavor for this smoothie was easy. And to make it creamy but still light in texture and calories, I added a big handful of frozen cauliflower and protein-rich yogurt. A touch of honey provided sweetness and brightened the flavors. When we introduced the smoothie alongside the Black Tap shake, people commented on the clean, fresh taste as they guzzled their smoothies down. Now even cotton candy can be guilt free!

Fat Bomb

Serves 1

Ingredients:

½ ripe avocado, pitted and peeled

1 serving chocolate protein powder*

1 tablespoon almond butter

1 tablespoon cacao powder

1 cup (240 ml) almond milk or milk of choice

4 ice cubes

Combine all the ingredients in a blender and blend until smooth.

This smoothie also works great for people on a ketogenic diet, if you use keto protein powder.

OPTIONAL SUPER BOOSTS:

BEE POLLEN

CHIA SEEDS

HEMP SEEDS

FLAX SEEDS

MACA POWDER

COLLAGEN PEPTIDES

MCT OIL

REISHI

ASHWAGANDHA

PROBIOTIC POWDER

GREENS POWDER

PINK HIMALAYAN SALT

BRAZIL NUTS

I often get asked by parents of underweight kids what they can feed them to help them gain weight in a nutritious way. This smoothie is one I like to recommend because it contains high-calorie fats, but they're nutrient-dense healthy fats that everyone should be eating. These types of fats help lower LDL cholesterol, are anti-inflammatory, and help our bodies store energy. They are essential to any well-balanced, healthy diet.

The luscious fats in this smoothie—avocado and almond butter—also help you to feel fuller longer, which is especially important for busy kids or anyone working out regularly. Every sip has a luscious chocolate flavor without additional sweeteners your body doesn't want or need.

Hubby's Dessert

Serves 1

Ingredients:

½ frozen banana, peeled

½ cup (80 g) frozen mango chunks

¼ cup (25 g) frozen coconut sheets or chunks

1 dried date, pitted

6 cashews raw, unsalted*

¼ teaspoon vanilla extract or ⅛ teaspoon vanilla paste

¾ cup (180 ml) almond milk or milk of choice

Combine all the ingredients in a blender and blend until smooth.

*If you don't have a high-powered blender, soak the cashews overnight (discard the water before using) to make them easier to puree perfectly smooth (see page 249).

OPTIONAL SUPER BOOSTS:

BEE POLLEN

CHIA SEEDS

HEMP SEEDS

FLAX SEEDS

MACA POWDER

VANILLA OR PLAIN PROTEIN POWDER

COLLAGEN PEPTIDES

REISHI

ASHWAGANDHA

PROBIOTIC POWDER

PINK HIMALAYAN SALT

BRAZIL NUTS

My husband often makes this one after dinner, thus its name. It's sweet enough to qualify as a dessert but healthy enough that you don't feel like you're being indulgent. With tropical notes from the banana, mango, and coconut, it's a soothing and delicious way to end the day.

Keto-Friendly Double Chocolate

Serves 1

Ingredients:

½ ripe avocado, pitted and peeled

1 tablespoon cacao powder

1 serving keto-friendly chocolate protein powder

1 tablespoon chia seeds

¼ cup (60 ml) full-fat coconut milk

¾ cup (180 ml) almond milk or milk of choice

Combine all the ingredients in a blender and blend until smooth.

OPTIONAL SUPER BOOSTS:

BEE POLLEN

CHIA SEEDS

HEMP SEEDS

FLAX SEEDS

MACA POWDER

COLLAGEN PEPTIDES

MCT OIL

SPIRULINA

CHLORELLA

REISHI

ASHWAGANDHA

PROBIOTIC POWDER

GREENS POWDER

PINK HIMALAYAN SALT

BRAZIL NUTS

I've never been one to regularly follow any specific diet, but I have friends who swear by their ketogenic experience of eating a high-fat, low-carb, sufficient protein diet, which results in the body burning fats instead of carbs. However, whether or not you're on a keto kick, this smoothie is a delicious way to go.

Peanut Butter Banana Date Shake

Serves 1

Ingredients:

1 frozen banana, peeled

2 dried dates, pitted

1 tablespoon peanut butter*

⅛ teaspoon ground cinnamon

1 tablespoon chia seeds

1 cup (240 ml) milk of choice

Combine all the ingredients in a blender and blend until smooth.

*I highly recommend using organic peanut butter, as peanuts are among the most heavily sprayed crops we eat and thus can be carcinogenic. In spite of their name, peanuts are not nuts, but rather legumes, which grow underground and lack the hard protective shells of nuts, causing them to easily become contaminated in the growing process. Organic foods are grown and made without the use of pesticides and other chemicals. If you have a peanut allergy, substitute any of your favorite nut or seed butters for peanut butter.

OPTIONAL SUPER BOOSTS:

BEE POLLEN

HEMP SEEDS

FLAX SEEDS

MACA POWDER

VANILLA OR PLAIN PROTEIN POWDER

COLLAGEN PEPTIDES

REISHI

ASHWAGANDHA

PROBIOTIC POWDER

PINK HIMALAYAN SALT

BRAZIL NUTS

When it comes to the foods I almost always have on hand, peanut butter is at the top of the list. Not so surprising since I have three kids. I use it in sandwiches, as a heaping spoonful when one of us is starving and needs a protein pick-me-up, and for smoothies—especially in this shake. The dates lend a nice caramel note, while the chia seeds add a punch of omega-3 fatty acids and protein. It's a smoothie you'll suck down so fast all you'll be left with is the craving to have it again as soon as possible.

An irresistible taste that will appeal to you no matter what your age

PB&J

Ingredients:

½ fresh or frozen banana, peeled

¾ cup (112 g) fresh or frozen strawberries

1 tablespoon peanut butter (salted or unsalted)*

1 dried date, pitted

1 tablespoon goji berries

1 cup (240 ml) milk of choice

Combine all the ingredients in a blender and blend until smooth.

If you have a peanut allergy, substitute any of your favorite nut or seed butters for the peanut butter.

OPTIONAL SUPER BOOSTS:

BEE POLLEN

CHIA SEEDS

HEMP SEEDS

FLAX SEEDS

MACA POWDER

VANILLA OR PLAIN PROTEIN POWDER

COLLAGEN PEPTIDES

REISHI

ASHWAGANDHA

PROBIOTIC POWDER

PINK HIMALAYAN SALT

BRAZIL NUTS

GOLDEN BERRIES

Show me a kid (or adult, for that matter) who doesn't love the combination of peanut butter and jelly, and I'll make them a believer after tasting this beauty. I usually have unsalted peanut butter on hand, but when I made this smoothie with roasted salted peanut butter, it was a totally different but equally mouthwatering experience. The slight saltiness of the peanut butter mixed with the sweet strawberries and vitamin C– and iron-rich goji berries give this smoothie an irresistible taste that will appeal to you no matter what your age. Add a few frozen cauliflower florets to get a vegetable in and make it even creamier.

Samoa

Serves 1

Ingredients:

1 fresh or frozen banana, peeled

¼ cup (33 g) frozen cauliflower florets

¼ cup (25 g) frozen coconut sheets or chunks

1 serving chocolate protein powder*

1 dried date, pitted

¼ teaspoon vanilla extract or ⅛ teaspoon vanilla paste

¾ cup (180 ml) coconut milk

Toppings (optional): cacao nibs, unsweetened coconut

Combine all the ingredients in a blender and blend until smooth. Pour into a serving glass and add your choice of toppings.

*For a deeper chocolate flavor, replace the chocolate protein powder with 2 teaspoons cacao powder.

OPTIONAL SUPER BOOSTS:

BEE POLLEN

CHIA SEEDS

HEMP SEEDS

FLAX SEEDS

MACA POWDER

COLLAGEN PEPTIDES

MCT OIL

REISHI

ASHWAGANDHA

PROBIOTIC POWDER

PINK HIMALAYAN SALT

BRAZIL NUTS

I will always have a soft spot for Girl Scout Cookies. I love what the organization does to encourage confidence, courage, and character for girls, but also for the delectable cookies they sell to raise the funds needed to support the organization. If you forced me to pick a favorite, it would have to be Samoas. There's something about the combination of chocolate, caramel, and coconut (especially when frozen) that makes them truly addictive. The first time I made this Samoa-inspired smoothie, I refrained from telling my kids what it was based on, but within two sips they knew exactly what it was.

Super Seed

Serves 1

Ingredients:

½ fresh or frozen banana, peeled

¼ cup (33 g) frozen cauliflower florets

1 tablespoon sunflower seed butter

1 tablespoon raw pumpkin seeds

1 tablespoon hemp seeds

1 tablespoon chia seeds

1 serving protein powder

¾ cup (180 ml) coconut milk or milk of choice

2 ice cubes

Combine all the ingredients in a blender and blend until smooth.

OPTIONAL SUPER BOOSTS:

BEE POLLEN

FLAX SEEDS

MACA POWDER

COLLAGEN PEPTIDES

REISHI

ASHWAGANDHA

PROBIOTIC POWDER

PINK HIMALAYAN SALT

BRAZIL NUTS

One of my earliest memories is sitting with my grandfather in his backyard and him teaching me how to open sunflower seed shells with my teeth. We'd go through pounds of these protein- and vitamin E–packed morsels in a sitting.

Most seeds, like chia and hemp, are rich in omega-3 fatty acids and fiber, and I make sure to add them to most smoothies. Then one day it came to me to create a smoothie based almost entirely on seeds. It's an easy one to whip up, especially if you're a seed connoisseur like me, who keeps labeled jars of seeds in the freezer year-round. You can vary the types of seeds based on what you have on hand, but the combination in this recipe adds not only a ton of flavor, but also vitamins, minerals, and nutrients.

Halva

Ingredients:

½ fresh or frozen banana, peeled

2 fresh figs

1 dried date, pitted

1 tablespoon tahini

¼ teaspoon vanilla extract or ⅛ teaspoon vanilla paste

1 cup (240 ml) milk of choice

Combine all the ingredients in a blender and blend until smooth.

OPTIONAL SUPER BOOSTS:

BEE POLLEN

CHIA SEEDS

HEMP SEEDS

FLAX SEEDS

MACA POWDER

VANILLA OR PLAIN PROTEIN POWDER

COLLAGEN PEPTIDES

REISHI

ASHWAGANDHA

PROBIOTIC POWDER

PINK HIMALAYAN SALT

BRAZIL NUTS

I can't pinpoint the exact first time I tried halva, a sweet, crumbly, sesame-flavored dessert, but I remember it made me absolutely weak in the knees. What was it? How did it achieve that incredible taste and unique texture? I was amazed to discover that it's basically made from just two simple ingredients, tahini and sugar or honey.

This nut-free, vegan smoothie tastes incredibly close to my beloved halva, and it's made with tahini (aka sesame paste), which can easily be found at your local market. The best part about this halva? It's made without any refined sugars, but is just as delicious as the dessert that inspired it.

healing +

supporting

Immunity Booster

Serves 1

Ingredients:

½ fresh or frozen banana, peeled

¼-inch (6-mm) piece fresh turmeric, peeled and chopped, or ¼ teaspoon ground turmeric

2 tablespoons plain or vanilla yogurt (preferably Greek)

½ cup (65 g) fresh or frozen mixed berries

1 handful fresh spinach

1 dried date, pitted or 2 teaspoons honey for added sweetness, if desired

2 teaspoons hemp seeds

1 teaspoon bee pollen

1 tablespoon almond or another nut butter

1 crack black pepper

½ cup (120 ml) almond milk

Combine all the ingredients in a blender and blend until smooth.

OPTIONAL SUPER BOOSTS:

CHIA SEEDS

FLAX SEEDS

MACA POWDER

VANILLA OR PLAIN PROTEIN POWDER

MCT OIL

REISHI

ASHWAGANDHA

PROBIOTIC POWDER

GOJI BERRIES

AÇAÍ POWDER

CAMU CAMU POWDER

PINK HIMALAYAN SALT

BRAZIL NUTS

GOLDEN BERRIES

As soon as fall begins, I start preparing for that time of year when everyone seems to fall prey to cold and flu season. Instead of stocking up on bottles of vitamins and kids' multi-gummies, I start reinforcing our immune systems with tons of resistance-building foods. This smoothie is loaded with vitamins, antioxidants, and superfoods that kick your immune system into overdrive, improve your gut health, and even help you feel better if you've already succumbed to the worst the season has to offer.

Antioxidant Rich

Ingredients:

½ cup (74 g) fresh or frozen blueberries

½ cup (75 g) fresh or frozen strawberries

½ cup (65 g) fresh or frozen raspberries

2 fresh kale leaves, thick stems removed, chopped

1 dried date, pitted

1 tablespoon cacao powder

1 tablespoon goji berries

¾ cup (180 ml) milk of choice

Combine all the ingredients in a blender and blend until smooth.

OPTIONAL SUPER BOOSTS:

BEE POLLEN

HEMP SEEDS

CHIA SEEDS

COLLAGEN PEPTIDES

REISHI

ASHWAGANDHA

GOLDEN BERRIES

Antioxidants aid the defense of our cells by inhibiting oxidation and the production of potentially harmful molecules known as free radicals, shown by many studies to contribute to the aging process. Certain foods, such as chocolate, berries, goji berries, and kale contain high levels of antioxidants. They also happen to be the stars of this smoothie, an antioxidant-a-palooza that's a smart way to start your day. Your cells will thank you.

Your cells will

thank you

Bright Blue

Serves 1

Ingredients:

½ fresh or frozen banana, peeled

⅓ cup (60 g) fresh or frozen mango chunks

¼ cup (33 g) frozen cauliflower florets

1 serving Blue Majik

1 tablespoon almond butter

1 teaspoon fresh lemon juice

¾ cup (180 ml) milk of choice

Combine all the ingredients in a blender and blend until smooth.

OPTIONAL SUPER BOOSTS:

BEE POLLEN

CHIA SEEDS

HEMP SEEDS

VANILLA OR PLAIN PROTEIN POWDER

COLLAGEN PEPTIDES

REISHI

ASHWAGANDHA

PROBIOTIC POWDER

PINK HIMALAYAN SALT

BRAZIL NUTS

My kids call this the Smurf smoothie on account of its intense blue color, which only enhances its drinkability in their eyes, but trust me when I say that you don't need to be a kid to love it.

The kid (and parent) in me rejoiced the day I discovered Blue Majik, a magical blue algae powder that is an extract of spirulina and can naturally turn food a shade of blue I had thought impossible. While you may cringe at the thought of putting algae in your smoothie, the taste is completely masked. And it delivers 24 percent of your daily iron, containing even more than spinach, and is believed to support joints and increase energy.

Divine Start

Serves 1

Ingredients:

½ cup (15 g) fresh spinach

2 fresh kale leaves, thick stems removed, chopped

½ fresh or frozen banana, peeled

2 tablespoons frozen coconut sheets or chunks

1 dried date, pitted

1 tablespoon chia seeds

1 tablespoon flax seeds or flaxseed meal

¾ cup (180 ml) coconut milk

Combine all the ingredients in a blender and blend until smooth.

OPTIONAL SUPER BOOSTS:

BEE POLLEN

HEMP SEEDS

COLLAGEN PEPTIDES

REISHI

ASHWAGANDHA

I'm a big believer that if you fill your body up with nourishing ingredients before anything else, you will feel it from head to toe. When you drink this green machine, you have all of your bases covered: a handful of kale and spinach for a mild greens flavor and a ton of antioxidants, banana and date for just the right amount of sweetness, chia seeds for protein and omega-3 fatty acids, flax seeds for fiber, and frozen coconut meat and coconut milk for healthy fat with plenty of coconut flavor.

It all comes together to help you glow all day long

Glow

Serves 1

Ingredients:

1 cup (30 g) fresh spinach

½ fresh or frozen banana, peeled

1 small Gala, Fuji, or other sweet apple, cored, seeded, and cut into chunks*

¼ lemon (with peel and pith), seeded

1 serving collagen peptides

½ cup (120 ml) coconut water or water

1 handful ice

Combine all the ingredients in a blender and blend until smooth.

If you don't have a high-powered blender, peel the apple.

OPTIONAL SUPER BOOSTS:

BEE POLLEN

CHIA SEEDS

HEMP SEEDS

FLAX SEEDS

VANILLA OR PLAIN PROTEIN POWDER

PROBIOTIC POWDER

If you drink this smoothie every day in place of whatever your current breakfast menu is, the positive effects will be felt pretty quickly. I include collagen in my smoothies every day, and my hair, skin, and nails have never felt or looked so good. Adding lemon with the peel not only gives this smoothie extra flavor and zip, but it enhances its detoxifying potency. The natural sweetness of apple, fiber- and nutrient-dense spinach, and hydrating coconut water round out the mix, and it all comes together to help you glow all day long.

Golden Milk

Serves 1

Ingredients:

½ fresh or frozen banana, peeled

½ cup (80 g) fresh or frozen mango chunks

¼ cup (33 g) frozen cauliflower florets

½-inch (1.25-cm) piece fresh turmeric, peeled and chopped, or ¼ teaspoon ground turmeric

1 tablespoon honey or maple syrup

2 teaspoons coconut oil

¼ teaspoon ground cinnamon

1 pinch freshly ground black pepper

¾ cup (180 ml) milk of choice

Combine all the ingredients in a blender and blend until smooth.

OPTIONAL SUPER BOOSTS:

BEE POLLEN

VANILLA PROTEIN POWDER

CHIA SEEDS

COLLAGEN PEPTIDES

REISHI

ASHWAGANDHA

Golden milks are all the rage now, but the truth is that people have been drinking them for centuries—and for good reason. Golden milk is basically any kind of milk with turmeric, black pepper, and a fat—with the latter two ingredients increasing the bioavailability of turmeric's powerful healing compounds.

I take the classic drink a step further to turn it into a smoothie. Frozen mango and banana lend it a tropical bent, not to mention the added benefit of potassium, vitamin C, and other immunity-boosting nutrients. Cinnamon and turmeric give warmth and depth of flavor to the drink. If you're looking for anti-inflammatory, antioxidant, and digestion benefits, this smoothie is the one.

Muscle Builder

Serves 1

Ingredients:

½ fresh or frozen banana, peeled

½ cup (74 g) frozen blueberries

1 tablespoon almond butter

1 serving plant-based protein powder

1 tablespoon hemp seeds

¾ cup (180 ml) milk of choice

Combine all the ingredients in a blender and blend until smooth.

OPTIONAL SUPER BOOSTS:

BEE POLLEN

CHIA SEEDS

FLAX SEEDS

MACA POWDER

COLLAGEN PEPTIDES

MCT OIL

SPIRULINA

CHLORELLA

REISHI

ASHWAGANDHA

PROBIOTIC POWDER

GREENS POWDER

GOJI BERRIES

AÇAÍ POWDER

CAMU CAMU POWDER

MAQUI BERRY POWDER

PINK HIMALAYAN SALT

BRAZIL NUTS

I'm a total movie junkie. There's little I love to do more than a weekend double feature at our local theater. Instead of heading for the popcorn and candy beforehand, I usually pop into the smoothie shop next door to fill myself up with something delicious and creamy. The smoothie shop's menu is geared entirely for the nearby gym, and one of their best options inspired this recipe.

Whether you are building muscle or burning fat, you need to consume plenty of protein. I add a variety of types here—hemp seeds, almond butter, and protein powder—not only for taste, but also for their variety of nutrients. You can adjust the flavor in the smoothie by using vanilla or chocolate protein powder or a neutral flavor to let the blueberry really shine through.

Skin Brightener

Serves 1

Ingredients:

½ fresh or frozen banana, peeled

½ ripe avocado, pitted and peeled

½ cup (80 g) fresh or frozen pineapple chunks

1 dried date, pitted

1 serving collagen peptides

2 teaspoons fresh lemon juice

½-inch (1.25-cm) piece fresh ginger, peeled

1 tablespoon flax seeds or flaxseed meal

¾ cup (180 ml) water, coconut water,
or herbal tea

**Combine all the ingredients in a blender
and blend until smooth.**

OPTIONAL SUPER BOOSTS:

BEE POLLEN

CHIA SEEDS

HEMP SEEDS

FLAX SEEDS

MCT OIL

SPIRULINA

CHLORELLA

REISHI

ASHWAGANDHA

PROBIOTIC POWDER

GOJI BERRIES

AÇAÍ POWDER

CAMU CAMU POWDER

MAQUI BERRY POWDER

MACA POWDER

PINK HIMALAYAN SALT

BRAZIL NUTS

I remember spending time on the beaches of Florida when I was a little kid, my mother constantly begging me to cover my body—and especially my face—in sunscreen. Now, living with the effects of early sun damage, I wish I had listened to her more. I can't turn back the clock, but I can focus on drinking more water, exercise, being super vigilant with the SPF, and eating plenty of the foods that can help with skin elasticity.

Since I started adding collagen peptides to my daily smoothies several years ago, I can see the results. My skin looks brighter and plumper. The healthy fats in avocado help hydrate your skin, while adding a creamy texture to this smoothie. Mixed with other skin-supporting ingredients, this drink is the next best thing to turning back the clock.

The next best thing to
turning back the clock

Superfood

Serves 1

Ingredients:

½ cup (65 g) mixed fresh or frozen berries (strawberries, blackberries, raspberries, and/or blueberries)

½ fresh or frozen banana, peeled

2 fresh kale leaves, thick stems removed, chopped

½ cup (15 g) fresh spinach

¼ cup (60 ml) plain or vanilla Greek yogurt or kefir

½-inch (1.25-cm) piece fresh turmeric, peeled, or ¼ teaspoon ground turmeric

1 tablespoon coconut oil

1 tablespoon flax seeds or flaxseed meal

¾ cup (180 ml) milk of choice

Combine all the ingredients in a blender and blend until smooth.

OPTIONAL SUPER BOOSTS:

BEE POLLEN

CHIA SEEDS

HEMP SEEDS

VANILLA OR PLAIN PROTEIN POWDER

COLLAGEN PEPTIDES

MCT OIL

REISHI

ASHWAGANDHA

PROBIOTIC POWDER

GREENS POWDER

GOJI BERRIES

AÇAÍ POWDER

CAMU CAMU POWDER

MAQUI BERRY POWDER

MACA POWDER

PINK HIMALAYAN SALT

BRAZIL NUTS

GOLDEN BERRIES

There's no one food that holds the key to good health or disease prevention, but when you come up with the right combination of nutrient-dense foods in one glass, you can get a little closer to the bull's-eye. Dark leafy greens, berries, seeds, kefir and yogurt, and turmeric are superfood all-stars, as they are rich in vitamins and minerals, which can help us ward off disease and live longer, healthier lives. Whiz them up in a blender and what results is a truly delicious smoothie that makes you feel super to boot. It's a win-win.

Tummy Soother

Serves 1

Ingredients:

1 cup (140 g) peeled, seeded, and chopped ripe papaya

½ teaspoon lime zest, grate before juicing

2 teaspoons fresh lime juice

½-inch (1.25-cm) piece fresh ginger, peeled

1 serving probiotic powder

1 pinch pink Himalayan salt

¾ cup (180 ml) coconut water

Combine all the ingredients in a blender and blend until smooth.

OPTIONAL SUPER BOOSTS:

BEE POLLEN

HEMP SEEDS

COLLAGEN PEPTIDES

It's truly magical how healing food can be. For many years, I would get awful stomachaches from stress and not eating as well as I should. The best remedy was papaya: I'd cut open a ripe one, give it a big squeeze of lime, and within minutes of eating it, I'd start to feel better. Papayas became a lifesaver for me, all because they contain an enzyme that aids digestion.

In this smoothie, papaya and lime are bolstered with electrolyte- and potassium-rich coconut water, fresh ginger to alleviate nausea, probiotic powder for adding good bacteria to your gut, and a pinch of Himalayan salt to help your body absorb all the nutrients. It's a delightfully refreshing smoothie that's yummy and good for the tummy.

Cherry Vanilla

Serves 1

Ingredients:

½ frozen banana, peeled

½ cup (40 g) fresh or frozen cherries, pitted

¼ cup (60 ml) vanilla Greek yogurt

1 serving vanilla protein powder

1 serving collagen peptides

¾ cup (180 ml) milk of choice

Combine all the ingredients in a blender and blend until smooth.

OPTIONAL SUPER BOOSTS:

BEE POLLEN

CHIA SEEDS

HEMP SEEDS

FLAX SEEDS

MCT OIL

REISHI

ASHWAGANDHA

PROBIOTIC POWDER

GOJI BERRIES

BRAZIL NUTS

When I taste anything with artificial cherry flavoring, it makes me nauseous (I think I associate it with the vile-flavored cough syrup of my youth). However, give me a bowl of fresh cherries and it's a completely different story. The same goes for my smoothies. Cherries, whether they're fresh or frozen, give this smoothie a burst of deep natural sweetness. Believe it or not, they are also one of the few natural sources of melatonin, making this smoothie a perfect after-dinner treat if you're looking to get more z's. You can add ¼ cup (33 g) frozen cauliflower, fresh kale, or spinach to get a vegetable in.

The Kitchen Sink

Serves 1

Ingredients:

½ fresh or frozen banana, peeled

¾ cup (112 g) frozen strawberries, mango, raspberries, and/or blueberries

½ cup (15 g) spinach, stemmed and chopped kale, chopped baked sweet potato (without peel), chopped zucchini, and/or raw chopped carrot

1 serving protein powder (any type)

1 serving collagen peptides

1 tablespoon hemp or chia seeds

¾ cup (180 ml) milk of choice

Combine all the ingredients in a blender and blend until smooth.

OPTIONAL SUPER BOOSTS:

BEE POLLEN

FLAX SEEDS

MCT OIL

SPIRULINA

CHLORELLA

REISHI

ASHWAGANDHA

PROBIOTIC POWDER

GREENS POWDER

GOJI BERRIES

AÇAÍ POWDER

CAMU CAMU POWDER

MAQUIBERRY POWDER

MACA POWDER

PINK HIMALAYAN SALT

BRAZIL NUTS

GOLDEN BERRIES

I often get asked about the proportions of a typical smoothie. In my experience, there's not a cut-and-dry answer. Years after making a different kind of smoothie almost every day, I still find myself discovering incredible new variations based on different combinations of fruits, vegetables, proteins, and carbohydrates. The excitement derived from that process is what makes smoothie making (and drinking) so much fun for me. I love knowing there's always a new and tasty way you can feed your body what it needs in one glass. You have a lot of flexibility with what you can put in it, and you can feel free to tailor it to your cravings and/or whatever ingredients you've got on hand. Be the master chef of your own creation.

Everything But Banana

Serves 1

Ingredients:

½ ripe avocado, pitted and peeled

1 dried date, pitted

⅓ cup (60 g) frozen mango chunks

⅓ cup (50 g) frozen strawberries

1 small carrot, peeled and chopped
(about ¼ cup/32 g)

1 teaspoon camu camu powder

2 tablespoons kefir

1 tablespoon hemp seeds

4 cashews raw, unsalted*

1 teaspoon bee pollen

¾ cup (180 ml) milk of choice

Combine all the ingredients in a blender and blend until smooth.

*If you don't have a high-powered blender, soak the cashews overnight (discard the water before using) to make them easier to puree perfectly smooth (see page 249).

OPTIONAL SUPER BOOSTS:

CHIA SEEDS

FLAX SEEDS

VANILLA OR PLAIN PROTEIN POWDER

COLLAGEN PEPTIDES

MCT OIL

REISHI

ASHWAGANDHA

PROBIOTIC POWDER

GREENS POWDER

GOJI BERRIES

AÇAÍ POWDER

MAQUI BERRY POWDER

MACA POWDER

PINK HIMALAYAN SALT

BRAZIL NUTS

GOLDEN BERRIES

While it may be hard to believe, there are actually people who don't like bananas. Whenever I post a smoothie recipe on Weelicious, without fail I get readers asking for banana-free options. Of course, I oblige. This one is thick, creamy, and sweet from a combination of avocado, frozen mango, strawberries, and raw carrot. And if you're someone who can't imagine a smoothie without banana, trust me, you won't miss the banana a bit!

seasonal

Orange Sunshine

Serves 1

Ingredients:

½ frozen banana, peeled

1 orange, peeled and chopped (try to remove as much of the white pith as possible so it's not bitter)

⅓ cup (70 ml) vanilla or plain Greek yogurt (dairy-free yogurt works too)*

½ cup (120 ml) orange juice or milk of choice

¼ teaspoon vanilla extract or ⅛ teaspoon vanilla paste

3 ice cubes

Combine all the ingredients in a blender and blend until smooth.

*If using plain yogurt, you can add 2 teaspoons honey to sweeten it.

When it's cold in Kentucky, there isn't a ton for a teenager to do, so in order to stay out of trouble, my friends and I became regulars at our local mall. We would shop (not that we were actually buying much), go to the movies, and grab an Orange Julius. Made primarily with sugar, orange juice concentrate, milk, and vanilla, that sugar bomb masquerading as a citrus drink was considered to be healthy by us young'uns.

Here I create my own healthy version to satisfy a nostalgic obsession and for a taste of sunshine on a cold, gloomy day. It has plenty of protein and probiotics from the Greek yogurt, vitamin C and fiber from the fresh orange, and potassium from the banana. If you want to replicate the original's extra frothy top so you can acquire a citrus mustache when sipping, let it go in the blender a little longer than usual.

Blueberry Muffin

Serves 1

Ingredients:

½ cup (74 g) fresh or frozen blueberries

½ fresh or frozen banana, peeled

½ cup (120 ml) plain or vanilla Greek yogurt

¼ cup (20 g) old-fashioned oats

¼ teaspoon lemon zest

½ cup (120 ml) milk of choice

Combine all the ingredients in a blender and blend until smooth.

OPTIONAL SUPER BOOSTS:

BEE POLLEN

CHIA SEEDS

HEMP SEEDS

FLAX SEEDS

MACA POWDER

VANILLA OR PLAIN PROTEIN POWDER

COLLAGEN PEPTIDES

PROBIOTIC POWDER

PINK HIMALAYAN SALT

BRAZIL NUTS

From kindergarten through eighth grade I was always the first kid picked up by the school bus and the last one dropped off, all part of my hour-plus commute to and from school. My mom used to get up at the crack of dawn in order to give me a bowl of cereal and milk, but on the occasions she felt inspired, she'd have warm blueberry muffins awaiting me, the taste and smell of which are still imprinted on me.

I'm bringing the blueberry muffin back for breakfast, only with a Smoothie Project spin. It mimics the flavors of everyone's favorite muffin, only it's chock-full of ingredients any kid (or adult) should be eating. I particularly like to make this smoothie when wild blueberries are in season.

Cherry Almond

Serves 1

Ingredients:

½ fresh or frozen banana, peeled

½ cup (76 g) fresh or frozen cherries, pitted

¼ cup (33 g) frozen cauliflower florets

1 tablespoon almond butter

¾ cup (180 ml) almond milk

Combine all the ingredients in a blender and blend until smooth.

OPTIONAL SUPER BOOSTS:

BEE POLLEN

CHIA SEEDS

HEMP SEEDS

FLAX SEEDS

MACA POWDER

VANILLA OR PLAIN PROTEIN POWDER

COLLAGEN PEPTIDES

MCT OIL

REISHI

ASHWAGANDHA

PROBIOTIC POWDER

GOJI BERRIES

AÇAÍ POWDER

CAMU CAMU POWDER

PINK HIMALAYAN SALT

BRAZIL NUTS

In my visits to smoothie shops, I've tasted my fair share of chalky smoothies. I once ordered a cherry smoothie and was taken aback by its gritty texture and cloying, artificial cherry flavor. As a food professional, I approach making smoothies the same way I approach cooking anything—it's all about utilizing the best ingredients possible to achieve the most delicious result. Using fresh cherries when they are in season is definitely one way to do that. However, as long as you use good frozen cherries, you can make this summer flavor year-round.

This smoothie is as pure, fresh, and balanced as they come. With only five ingredients, it's really simple to whip up, and since cherries are loaded with antioxidants and are a good source of fiber, there's a lot to like about this one.

Peach Protein Boost

Serves 1

Ingredients:

1 cup (160 g) fresh or frozen peach slices

1 dried date, pitted

1 tablespoon flax seeds or flaxseed meal

1 tablespoon chia seeds

1 serving vanilla or plain protein powder

1 cup (240 ml) almond milk

Combine all the ingredients in a blender and blend until smooth.

OPTIONAL SUPER BOOSTS:

BEE POLLEN

CHIA SEEDS

HEMP SEEDS

COLLAGEN PEPTIDES

PROBIOTIC POWDER

GOJI BERRIES

BRAZIL NUTS

Many years ago, I started buying peaches at our farmers' market from the peach ladies, as I affectionately call the gals from Tenerelli Orchards. To this day I don't think I've ever tasted anything as mouthwatering as the peaches that grow on their trees. The peach ladies also let me buy their "seconds" (meaning their bruised stock), which I slice up and freeze so that we can continue to enjoy them in our smoothies for months after peach season ends.

I let the peaches speak for themselves in this smoothie, added a date for a sweet caramel note, and incorporated flax, chia, and protein powder to make sure you stay nice and full. Whether you're able to get fresh peaches from your farmers' market or frozen from the grocery, it's all good. This is a smoothie that invites you to enjoy summer produce all year long.

White Peach Mango

Serves 1

Ingredients:

1 small white peach, pitted

½ cup (80 g) frozen mango chunks

1 tablespoon hemp seeds

1 pinch ground cardamom

¾ cup (180 ml) milk of choice

Combine all the ingredients in a blender and blend until smooth.

OPTIONAL SUPER BOOSTS:

BEE POLLEN

CHIA SEEDS

FLAX SEEDS

MACA POWDER

VANILLA OR PLAIN PROTEIN POWDER

COLLAGEN PEPTIDES

When white peaches are in season I buy them by the flat. While I'd have a hard time deciding on my favorite variety of peach, I can say that the whites make the most naturally sweet base for smoothies you've ever tasted. They're truly a unique fruit jewel and one that works well with almost any fruit or vegetable you pair with it. As peaches are rich, aromatic, and sweet in their own right, there's no need for banana in this smoothie. I add frozen mango to make it cool and enhance the thickness, but feel free to use a handful of ice instead. It's perfectly refreshing on a warm summer day.

Stone Fruit

Serves 1

Ingredients:

½ cup (80 g) fresh or frozen peach slices*

1 small plum, pitted and chopped*

½ fresh or frozen banana, peeled

2 fresh basil leaves

1 tablespoon hemp seeds

¾ cup (180 ml) milk of choice

Combine all the ingredients in a blender and blend until smooth.

If using fresh peaches and plums, add a handful of ice to the blender.

OPTIONAL SUPER BOOSTS:

BEE POLLEN

CHIA SEEDS

FLAX SEEDS

MACA POWDER

VANILLA OR PLAIN PROTEIN POWDER

COLLAGEN PEPTIDES

PROBIOTIC POWDER

PINK HIMALAYAN SALT

BRAZIL NUTS

When making smoothies, I try to be conscious of what's in season because at-peak produce not only tastes better, but it's also easier to find at a lower prices—which is especially important when it comes to pricier organic produce.

I was originally inspired to make this smoothie after witnessing my son's rapturous reaction to bite after bite of a stone fruit, basil, and burrata salad at a restaurant. The fresh basil here gives the flavor of the stone fruit a real pop.

Stone fruit is high in vitamins A and C, fiber, and potassium as well as being naturally sweet. If you can't get your hands on plums or peaches, you can substitute fresh apricots or nectarines with equal success.

The kind of smoothie you'd

picture drinking in Santorini

on a gorgeous summer day

Fig-tastic

Serves 1

Ingredients:

½ frozen banana, peeled

4 fresh or frozen figs

¼ cup (60 ml) plain or vanilla Greek yogurt

1 tablespoon honey

½ cup (120 ml) milk of choice

Combine all the ingredients in a blender and blend until smooth.

OPTIONAL SUPER BOOSTS:

BEE POLLEN

CHIA SEEDS

HEMP SEEDS

FLAX SEEDS

MACA POWDER

VANILLA OR PLAIN PROTEIN POWDER

COLLAGEN PEPTIDES

PROBIOTIC POWDER

PINK HIMALAYAN SALT

BRAZIL NUTS

There's a vendor at our farmers' market who trades in the most insanely delicious Greek yogurt. As soon as you walk up to his stand, he plies you with massive sample spoonfuls of his luscious, thick yogurt, which leaves me practically cross-eyed with elation. It comes in every flavor under the sun, from sour cherry to lemon to mango. My hands-down favorite is the fresh fig, and when figs are in season, you must buy a pint to make this smoothie.

You can make this smoothie with any Greek yogurt and with either super ripe fresh figs in summer or frozen figs with equal success. It's the kind of smoothie you'd picture drinking in Santorini on a gorgeous summer day.

Melon Cooler

Serves 1

Ingredients:

1 cup (160 g) peeled, seeded, and chopped ripe cantaloupe or honeydew melon

1 Persian cucumber, peeled and chopped

¼ cup (37 g) green grapes

1 serving collagen peptides

1 handful ice

¼ cup (60 ml) coconut milk or coconut water

Combine all the ingredients in a blender and blend until smooth.

OPTIONAL SUPER BOOSTS:

BEE POLLEN

HEMP SEEDS

VANILLA OR PLAIN PROTEIN POWDER

PROBIOTIC POWDER

PINK HIMALAYAN SALT

I go melon crazy from June through August, using the fruit for everything from making melons balls to go in camp lunch, to skewering cherry tomatoes and watermelon for kebabs, to wrapping wedges in prosciutto and drizzling them with pesto. And any leftover melon goes straight into the blender to make this smoothie.

You can use cantaloupe for an orange smoothie or honeydew for a green smoothie. They are rich in electrolytes, including potassium, sodium, and calcium, which your body needs to hydrate properly after a strenuous workout. The juice that comes out of the melon is comprised of 90 percent water, keeping the caloric intake low but the flavor intensely sweet. Note that it's important to wash melons with soap and water to remove unwanted bacteria before cutting into them.

Watermelon Chia

Serves 1

Ingredients:

1 cup (150 g) watermelon chunks, seeds removed

¼ cup (37 g) frozen strawberries

¼ cup (33 g) frozen cauliflower florets

2 fresh mint leaves

1 tablespoon chia seeds

½ cup (120 ml) coconut water, herbal iced tea, or milk of choice

Combine all the ingredients in a blender and blend until smooth.

OPTIONAL SUPER BOOSTS:

BEE POLLEN

HEMP SEEDS

FLAX SEEDS

MACA POWDER

VANILLA OR PLAIN PROTEIN POWDER

COLLAGEN PEPTIDES

PROBIOTIC POWDER

GOJI BERRIES

PINK HIMALAYAN SALT

In the summer when I load up my timeworn farmers' market cart, it's not unusual for at least ten pounds of my booty to be watermelon. We eat them at a dizzying pace in our house, but our eyes are often bigger than our bellies and we end up with leftovers. Sometimes I turn the remainder into watermelon juice. Other times I puree it, pour it into ice pop molds, and store it in the freezer. But the most memorable recipe I make with it is this smoothie.

Watermelon contains natural sugars and plenty of liquid, which make this smoothie light and refreshing. The fresh mint give it that je ne sais quoi that you might not be able to pinpoint right away, but which makes the flavor a total standout.

Apple Pie

Serves 1

Ingredients:

1 Gala, Fuji, or other sweet apple, cored, seeded, and cut into chunks*

½ cup (120 ml) plain or vanilla yogurt (vegan yogurt works too)

2 tablespoons old-fashioned oats

4 raw walnut halves

1 dried date, pitted

1 tablespoon chia seeds

½ teaspoon ground cinnamon

¼ cup (60 ml) milk of choice

¼ cup ice

Combine all the ingredients in a blender and blend until smooth.

If you don't have a high-powered blender, peel the apple.

OPTIONAL SUPER BOOSTS:

BEE POLLEN

HEMP SEEDS

FLAX SEEDS

MACA POWDER

VANILLA OR PLAIN PROTEIN POWDER

COLLAGEN PEPTIDES

REISHI

ASHWAGANDHA

PROBIOTIC POWDER

PINK HIMALAYAN SALT

BRAZIL NUTS

Months before a new season arrives, I'm already plotting new recipes for my smoothie kitchen. Last summer, I was craving the return of tart, crisp apples, which I love to snack on; add to smoothies, salads, and oatmeal; and use to make one of my favorite desserts, apple pie. Eating apple pie as frequently as I might like probably isn't the best idea, but this smoothie sates my cravings in the most healthful way possible. You'll be amazed at how well the classic flavors of apple pie translate to sipping through a straw.

This smoothie sates my cravings in the most healthful way possible

Autumn

Serves 1

Ingredients:

½ cup (125 g) sweet potato puree

½ Fuji, Gala, or other sweet apple, cored, seeded, and cut into chunks*

4 raw walnut halves

1 tablespoon flax seeds or flaxseed meal

¼ teaspoon pumpkin pie spice

½ cup (120 ml) milk of choice

1 handful ice

Combine all the ingredients in a blender and blend until smooth.

If you don't have a high-powered blender, peel the apple.

OPTIONAL SUPER BOOSTS:

BEE POLLEN

HEMP SEEDS

MACA POWDER

VANILLA OR PLAIN PROTEIN POWDER

COLLAGEN PEPTIDES

REISHI

ASHWAGANDHA

PROBIOTIC POWDER

PINK HIMALAYAN SALT

BRAZIL NUTS

Come fall, there are always two foods you can find in my kitchen: apples and sweet potatoes. At the start of any given week, I will bake up eight or so garnet yams or sweet potatoes to have on hand for snacks during the week or to pop in my smoothies. Apples and sweet potatoes are both nutritional powerhouses that have just the right amount of sweetness, making them the ideal smoothie ingredients. With their high levels of fiber and vitamin C and a flavor that pairs beautifully with other fruits and vegetables, apples are as versatile as they come, and studies have shown their contributions to overall neurological health. Sweet potatoes are loaded with vitamin A, help boost immunity, and add a silky texture to this smoothie.

If you have extra sweet potato, scoop it into silicone ice cube trays and freeze it for use in future smoothies. Then you'll be able to re-create the flavor of autumn any time of year!

Pumpkin Pie

Serves 1

Ingredients:

⅓ cup (73 g) pumpkin puree

½ fresh or frozen banana, peeled

¼ cup (33 g) frozen cauliflower florets

¼ teaspoon pumpkin pie spice

1 tablespoon maple syrup

¾ cup (180 ml) milk of choice

Combine all the ingredients in a blender and blend until smooth.

OPTIONAL SUPER BOOSTS:

BEE POLLEN

CHIA SEEDS

HEMP SEEDS

FLAX SEEDS

MACA POWDER

VANILLA OR PLAIN PROTEIN POWDER

COLLAGEN PEPTIDES

PROBIOTIC POWDER

PINK HIMALAYAN SALT

BRAZIL NUTS

Every year I wait for 364 days until the magic one arrives when I get to indulge in one of my all-time favorite desserts: pumpkin pie. I dream of the smooth texture and the warm mix of spices. Whenever I make pumpkin pie, bread, or muffins, I steal a big scoop of puree and use it to make this smoothie. With hints of cinnamon, nutmeg, ginger, and clove in every sip, it will scratch that pumpkin pie itch. And while I love fresh pumpkin, it can be time-consuming to roast a whole one, so I always have plenty of cans of pumpkin puree on hand.

Pumpkin Spice Latte

Serves 1

Ingredients:

3 tablespoon pumpkin puree

½ frozen banana, peeled

¼ teaspoon pumpkin pie spice

¼ teaspoon vanilla extract or ⅛ teaspoon vanilla paste

1 dried date, pitted, or 2 teaspoons maple syrup

½ cup (120 ml) milk of choice

1 serving collagen peptides

¼ cup (60 ml) strong brewed coffee

Combine all the ingredients in a blender and blend until smooth.

OPTIONAL SUPER BOOSTS:

BEE POLLEN

CHIA SEEDS

HEMP SEEDS

FLAX SEEDS

MACA POWDER

MCT OIL

PROBIOTIC POWDER

PINK HIMALAYAN SALT

BRAZIL NUTS

Whoever first thought of combining pumpkin puree and coffee is a total genius in my book. But I'm here to let you in on a little secret: There's a serious hole in the market. That's why I'm introducing the pumpkin spice latte smoothie. Need I say more?

Cran-berry

Serves 1

Ingredients:

1 fresh or frozen banana, peeled

¼ cup (33 g) frozen raspberries

½ cup (75 g) frozen strawberries

2 tablespoons fresh or frozen cranberries

1 dried date, pitted

¾ cup (180 ml) milk of choice

Combine all the ingredients in a blender and blend until smooth.

OPTIONAL SUPER BOOSTS:

BEE POLLEN

CHIA SEEDS

HEMP SEEDS

VANILLA OR PLAIN PROTEIN POWDER

COLLAGEN PEPTIDES

MCT OIL

REISHI

ASHWAGANDHA

PROBIOTIC POWDER

GOJI BERRIES, MAQUI

PINK HIMALAYAN SALT

BRAZIL NUTS

My husband almost always adds a few frozen cranberries to his smoothies. That may seem unusual given their exceptionally tart and sour reputation, but you only need a few to reap their benefits, whether you add frozen or a few fresh when they're in season in the fall. Cranberries have just about the greatest antioxidant capacity of any fruit or vegetable, topped only by wild blueberries and barely by cultivated blues. I find that adding a few to your smoothie is a great way to get these nutritional jewels into your diet, because let's face it, aside from cranberry sauce, which none of us is eating regularly, there's not a ton of easy ways to do it.

Don't worry about the tartness factor because there are two other, sweeter berries—both chock-full of fiber and antioxidants—that dominate the flavor while still keeping this smoothie crantastic. You can even add ¼ cup (33 g) frozen cauliflower, fresh kale, or spinach to get a vegetable in.

Getting the Most Out of Your Ingredients

We are living in the Golden Age of smoothies. From fruits to vegetables to nuts to supplements, the options for what you can put in your smoothies have never been more abundant. However, sorting through all the information about how the myriad available ingredients work in your body can prove overwhelming.

The following pages dive into the nitty-gritty of selecting ingredients—using fresh vs. frozen produce, choosing which milks and other liquids are best for smoothie making, determining ingredients based on your age and/or health issue or goal, and much more.

The **Super Boosts and Other Key Smoothie Ingredients** chart on page 238 brings clarity and simplicity to smoothie making, explaining the nutritional benefits of many of those ingredients and supplements you see lining the shelves of the supermarket.

The goal of this section is to filter out all the noise and reinforce just how easy this life change can be.

What Your Body Needs, Age by Age

Smoothies are a convenient way to get the nutrition we need, starting from the time we take our first sip through every subsequent stage of life.

Nationally renowned nutritionist Keri Glassman MS, RDN, CDN is the author of four bestselling healthy living books and is as smoothie obsessed as I am. I rely on Keri's expert nutritional and clean-living advice, and I asked her to talk about what's essential for our bodies from birth through our golden years.

LITTLE KIDS (10 MONTHS TO 6 YEARS OLD)

Starting to introduce a variety of foods at this age can help create a lifelong love of fresh produce. Focus on a mix of fruits and vegetables, proteins (nuts, seeds), fats (avocado, coconut oil, nuts and seeds, whole-milk dairy, and/or plant-based alternatives to dairy), calcium (yogurt, milk, broccoli), iron (nuts and leafy greens), and probiotics for good bacteria and digestive health.

Given how common food allergies are these days, Keri suggests parents refer to the American Academy of Pediatrics when it comes to introducing nuts and stresses the importance of offering foods rich in omega-3 fatty acids, which she says are critical for proper brain development during childhood.

BIG KIDS (7 TO 12 YEARS OLD)

At this age, kids are spending more time with their friends, playing sports, and burning extra calories, and they can be easily distracted from eating the foods their bodies need most. Keri says drinking smoothies can be a great way for kids to rehydrate and get essential nourishment when they're on the go in the morning or even right after school, before afternoon activities. Add a variety of fruits, vegetables, proteins, and bee pollen to help boost immunity and prevent seasonal allergies.

Keri advocates taking stock of where your kids are falling short nutrient wise. Calcium? Antioxidants? Protein? Adding in fruits and veggies that they may not eat in whole-food form is pretty simple. And if they are carb kids and hate the sight of protein, she says that adding nut butters and protein powder can help in this area.

TEENS (13 TO 19 YEARS OLD)

"The hardest thing about teens and nutrition," says Keri, "is that they are developing and changing rapidly and need to pay even closer attention to nutrition. At the same time, they are asserting independence and don't necessarily want their parents' input."

Yes, these are the years that kids transition into becoming young adults, often start making their own meals, and have easier access to fast food and less nutritious choices, so it's more important than ever to fill them up on nutrient-dense foods. Keri gives her teenage son a smoothie every single morning as a way to ensure that no matter what he eats at school, much of his daily nutritional needs have already been met. She emphasizes the importance of good teen nutrition for both brain and body, and I think the breakdown she shares below should be required reading for anyone with teens living under their roof:

Brain: It's extremely important to be aware of how significantly the brain continues to develop and change during this stage of life. As such, brain health is crucial. Exercise, sufficient sleep, and good food choices are essential. The gut-brain connection is crucial for teens, and diet plays an enormous role in maintaining it. Omega-3s remain vitally important to brain function and development (walnuts and hemp and chia seeds are good options). Additionally, it's vital to note that brain health is connected to mood, and in today's world where teens are at a higher risk of anxiety and depression than in the past, the foods they eat, especially ones that contribute to inflammation, can have a significant impact on their susceptibility to mental health disorders. Since 2009, there have been numerous studies reporting inverse associations between diet quality and CMDs (common mental disorders), depression, and anxiety in adults, children, and adolescents.[3] Reducing sugar intake and eating foods rich in antioxidants are two powerful ways of combating inflammation and lowering the risk of these conditions.

Body: Bones only build until ages twenty to thirty; after that it's all maintenance. That makes building healthy bones during the teen years essential. Adding foods rich in calcium, protein, and vitamins C and E will help promote healthy bone growth.

Protein is also extremely important for growth and development, as it helps to build, repair, and maintain tissue in the body. Girls, especially when they start menstruating, may need to focus on getting more iron in their diets.

Hormones: Keri says that getting fats *from the proper sources* is important for hormonal development and function, and needed for absorption of vitamins A, D, E, and K. Some good sources are olive oil, avocado, coconut, fatty fish (like salmon), grass-fed organic meats, chia, and flax.

Behavior: Keri notes the science showing correlation between the high intake of sugar and both negative behavior and mood disorders. Encourage teens to limit the sugar they might not realize they're consuming (e.g., through drinks, condiments, sauces, and snack bars), and reserve their sugar intake for conscious indulgences and for fruit, where sugar occurs naturally, in conjunction with other vitamins and nutrients.

Keri cites the importance of teens fostering a healthy microbiome, which has a direct link to brain function and mood. Focus on foods with live probiotics like kefir, kimchi, unsweetened yogurt, sauerkraut, and miso.

Weight Changes: The teen years are a time of growth. Weight will increase and bodies change. Teens' bodies require the most energy consumption out of any age group, and Keri recommends keeping your teen's focus on consuming a wholesome, healthy diet full of vegetables, protein, healthy fats, and whole grains, rather than weight. Emphasize for teens the importance of nourishing their growth, explaining that this is what will allow them to grow into their healthiest body and mind.

3. *"So depression is an inflammatory disease, but where does the inflammation come from?" BMC Med, 9.12.13.*

Eating Issues: Eating issues often first tend to crop up during the teens, fueled by everything from social pressure to unhealthy body image messaging in media and advertising. Obviously unhealthy, it can also lay the groundwork for future health issues. Keri says that teens' bodies need nutrients to support pubertal growth and a long lifespan. She offers many suggestions for parents, like helping your teen begin to consider her current food habits (e.g., is she snacking out of an emotional state, or from a positive place like being social with friends or enjoying the snack or treat). Keri recommends a positive, esteem-bolstering approach, like encouraging teens to eat from an empowered place, rather than a place of restriction (e.g., say, "I can have those blueberries," rather than, "I shouldn't have that cookie"), having them focus on how incredible their bodies are and how many things it is capable of doing, and reminding them that feeling good about their eating habits will reflect in feeling good about themselves.

20s TO 30s

In today's always-connected, work-obsessed culture, this stage of life is particularly intense. Balancing time for oneself amid starting and building a career and family is no easy feat.

Protein: If your hectic lifestyle means skipping meals, you may fall short of your body's protein needs. Protein is essential for building muscle and keeping you satisfied, especially if you are exercising regularly.

Iron: We need iron for oxygen transport in our cells. Without it, we feel faint and fatigued. Women in their twenties are especially at risk for iron deficiency because iron is lost during menstruation every month. That's why the daily recommended intake (ages nineteen to fifty) of iron is more than double for women than men (men require 8 mg/day, women, 18 mg/day). And the Recommended Dietary Allowance for pregnant women jumps even higher—27 mg/day!

Calcium and Vitamin D: A woman's peak bone mass is reached by her early twenties, so pack in the calcium and vitamin D–rich foods while your bones are still storing those nutrients.

Folate: This B vitamin is absolutely essential to pregnancy, and building up stores takes a while. Folate (found in foods such as leafy greens, citrus, and beans) is particularly important during the first two to three weeks of pregnancy, when it's needed to develop the nervous system. Folate deficiencies during pregnancy can lead to serious problems, including premature birth and infants born with neural tube defects. The daily recommended amount for folate is 400 mcg for both men and women, but this need increases to 600 mcg for pregnant and lactating women.

Gut health: This remains important during this stage of life, when people are deep in their professional lives—working long hours, running around, traveling—and often starting families.

Everyone I know at this age wants to slow down the aging process. Adding nutrient-dense foods is key, as what you put inside really does show on the outside, particularly when it comes to skin brightening, hair growth, and vitality. I use collagen peptides for stronger hair, skin, and nails. Keri offers more important nutritional facts for living your best life in your forties:

Fiber: It's not your fault that your body may not look the way it did on your prom night. As we get older, our bodies become less sensitive to insulin. This leads to a buildup of fat, most noticeably in the form of that dreaded belly bulge. A fiber-rich diet is a great weapon in combatting weight gain, as fiber keeps you feeling full for longer. Fiber can also help combat chronic conditions we are at increased risk for as we age.

Calcium: Our aging bodies are unable to absorb calcium as efficiently as they once did, so it's important to increase the amount of calcium in our diets to help support strong, healthy bones. For women, signs of osteoporosis may begin right after menopause, so be sure to get a lot of calcium and vitamin D to stay ahead.

Water: One simple way to fight belly fat is to stay hydrated. Water fills you up, acting as a natural appetite suppressant, and also aids in upping your metabolism.

Skin health: Increase your intake of omega-3s to help fight inflammation of the skin. Smoothies made with walnuts and flax seeds are good for doing this. Vitamin C, present in citrus, helps increase collagen production in your skin to promote elasticity.

Hormonal balance: This is a big one for the forty set. Green veggies and healthy fats (especially coconut oil) are super important during these years. Be diligent about balancing your blood sugar, as blood sugar underpins hormonal balance. When we eat too much sugar or refined carbs, excess insulin is produced, which in turn increases the production of an enzyme called aromatase. Aromatase is the main enzyme responsible for estrogen creation, and if you have an imbalance of estrogen to progesterone, the imbalance may cause weight gain.

Overall gut health: Gut health never goes out of style. It's important to keep your gut in tip-top shape, as it's an important site for estrogen detoxification. What does that mean? The liver sends excess estrogen to the colon for removal from the body, but if you are constipated, this can slow down its exit. Not a good thing. Also, if bad bacteria rule your gut, they might be producing an enzyme called beta-glucuronidase, which uncouples estrogen from its bond in the gut and allows it to roam free. Again, not good.

60+:

As you age, you may experience decreased sensitivity to smell and taste, even a lack of appetite, which can make it harder to get all the nutrients that you need. As a result, consuming a diet rich in nutrients (especially micronutrients) becomes even more important. Additionally, for those on medications with side effects that have an adverse effect on appetite, eating a balanced diet rich in fruits, vegetables, omega-3 fatty acids, calcium, and hydrating liquids (as you may not feel as thirsty as you used to) is crucial.

Sleep can become challenging at this stage of life, so a diet that supports your ability to get a good night's rest is key. Reishi can be a great addition to help you feel calm and relaxed, and even support sleep.

The risk of osteoporosis is significantly higher in your sixties, so getting enough calcium remains crucial.

Finally, calorie needs can decline, so there's no room for wasted calories in your diet. Making sure your calories are as nutrient dense as possible is essential.

SMOOTHIE

HACK

Want to stay fuller longer? Add an extra scoop of protein powder, nut butter, collagen peptides, or some organic tofu to your smoothie.

What Your Body Needs to Achieve a Goal or Address a Health Concern

From addressing a particular ailment to making sure your baby is getting the nutrients he or she needs, certain types of ingredients can help you achieve your goals and get what you need from your smoothie.

Slimming Down

A smart smoothie regimen can help manage weight and take off excess pounds.

Whitney English Tabaie, MS, RDN, highlights the power of eating a wide variety fruits and vegetables, noting, "They are high in vitamins and phytochemicals that may reduce oxidative stress, which has been linked to diabetes, obesity, and other metabolic syndromes." It's also important to keep the following in mind:

Fiber: Fruits and vegetables are high in fiber, and English Tabaie explains how fiber is helpful for a weight management routine: "Fiber has been shown to slow digestion. This helps increase satiety (the feeling of fullness) after a meal. Staying fuller longer helps prevent snacking between meals and the intake of excess, unnecessary calories."

Calories: Most veggies are low calorie, and smoothie-friendly veggies such as dark leafy greens, broccoli, cauliflower, beets, carrots, and zucchini abound. Fruits on the whole have more calories than vegetables; however, berries (which are also high in fiber), peaches, apples, grapes, cucumbers, papaya, cantaloupe, honeydew melon, and watermelon are all low-calorie options, giving you a wide variety of flavors to produce light—yet still tasty!—smoothies. Choosing a no-calorie liquid for your smoothies, such as water,

herbal tea, or coffee, is a great slimming solution that will enable you to achieve the consistency you desire with no waistline worries.

Protein: Important for nutritional balance, look for healthy, lower-calorie protein options, such as almonds or cashews; pumpkin and chia seeds; and low-fat dairy (like milk or Greek yogurt).

SMOOTHIES TO SUPPORT:
Detox (p. 137), Super Greens (p. 72), Passion (p. 50); in general, the Clean and Clear chapter (pages 128 to 143) has many great low-calorie smoothies to choose from!

Pregnant and Nursing Women

When you're pregnant, especially in your second and third trimesters when you should be consuming an additional 350 to 500 calories per day, good nutrition is essential. Not only are you eating for two, you're exposing your new baby to a variety of foods you want them to fall in love with in the long run. Studies show that the foods you eat while pregnant can help your baby gravitate toward those flavors as they begin eating food. Be mindful to consume more protein, flax and other fiber-rich foods, calcium (dairy and yogurt), folate (spinach), beta-carotene (sweet potatoes), berries, avocados (healthy fat), broccoli and dark leafy greens (such as kale and spinach), and also increase liquid intake, especially when nursing, to aid milk production. See page 121 for a smoothie recipe tailored for pregnant and nursing moms, as well as my own pregnancy story that inspired its creation.

SMOOTHIES TO SUPPORT:
Pregnancy (p. 121), Açaí "Bowl" (p. 106), Berry Vanilla Shake (p. 109), Superfood (p. 189)

ADHD

Earlier I talked about the blessing of my finding Kelly Dorfman, a vanguard clinical nutritionist who uses nutrition to treat conditions associated with brain function. If you or someone you know has ADHD, her book *Cure Your Child with Food* is essential reading. Dorfman told me, "It's important to remember that ADHD is not one thing or even a particular condition. It is a symptom that can be from a great number of causes: allergy or other reactions, poor diet, irritants, auditory processing issues, memory challenges, anxiety, visual motor problems, slow processing speed, developmental delays, and so on. We call ADHD a diagnosis, even though it is a symptom, because there are drugs that treat the symptom. Sort of the way that coffee treats tiredness. Yes, it makes you less tired, temporarily, but it does not address the underlying cause. As a long-term solution, it falls short."

From a nutritional standpoint, this is eye-opening, as there is a great deal of research supporting both the beneficial and detrimental effects of various diets on many of the potential causes of ADHD. Dorfman pointed to one study[4] that found that 50 percent of kids with ADHD improved when common food reactors, such as dairy and gluten, were removed in a straightforward elimination diet. Food dyes, sugary foods, and foods with pesticides are also wise to avoid.

A diet rich in fruits, vegetables, protein, and vitamins can help control symptoms of attention deficit, but only if you avoid sugar, artificial flavors, and common allergens as well. Plant-based milks like almond, cashew, and coconut are good alternatives to cow's milk, as dairy can interfere with focus (as can products containing gluten, corn, and soy). Potentially helpful smoothie additions include lion's mane (for brain function and focus); Brazil nuts (rich in selenium); foods rich in omega-3 fatty acids (such as chia, flax, walnuts, dark leafy greens, and hemp seeds); foods rich in zinc (various seeds and nuts such as cashews, oats, almonds); magnesium (such as avocados, Brazil nuts, bananas, spinach, pumpkin seeds, and almonds) and iron (pumpkin seeds, nuts, and leafy greens).

SMOOTHIES TO SUPPORT:
You're Nuts! (p. 145) and Super Seed (p.169)

Eczema

When it comes to diet and eczema, it's generally more about avoiding certain foods than what ingredients to add to your smoothie. Dairy, eggs, wheat or gluten, soy products, sugary foods, citrus, and certain spices and/or nuts can all be triggers for eczema. Probiotic foods such as yogurt and kefir (unless you have a flare up after eating) can also be beneficial as well as healthy fats like avocado, seeds and nuts, fruits such as berries, a variety of vegetables, and leafy greens. To ascertain what your particular sensitivities may be, try an elimination diet by removing potentially offending foods from your diet one at a time for five to seven days.

SMOOTHIES TO SUPPORT:
Blueberry Muffin Smoothie (p. 200), Divine Start (p. 178), Chocolate Avocado (use non-dairy milk) (p. 91)

4. *"Effects of a restricted elimination diet on the behaviour of children with attention-deficit hyperactivity disorder (INCA study): a randomised controlled trial, The Lancet, Feb 5–11, 2011*

Anxiety and Stress

"What we eat plays a major role in our psychological and emotional well-being," says English Tabaie. "Studies have shown that diets low in micronutrients and phytochemicals and high in calories, processed sugar, and saturated fat are associated with chronic inflammation, gut microbiome imbalance, and oxidative stress—all things associated with mood disorders." You can use smoothies as a tool to improve your mental health by including foods high in brain-boosting nutrients such as the following:

NUTRIENT	SOURCES
Omega-3 Fatty Acids	walnuts, chia seeds, flax seeds, hemp seeds
Zinc	pepitas (pumpkin seeds), beans, grains, nuts, seeds
Curcumin	turmeric
Selenium	Brazil nuts
Flavanoids	maca

ANTIOXIDANTS	SOURCES
Catechine	green tea (matcha)
Anthocyanins	berries
Procyanidins	cocoa (dark chocolate)
Resveratrol	peanuts, pistachios, grapes, blueberries, dark chocolate, cranberries

SMOOTHIES TO SUPPORT: Blue Chia (p. 113), Orange Sunshine (p. 199), Green Goddess (p. 68)

Digestion/Gastrointestinal Problems

The digestive tract plays a vital role in your health, as it's responsible for absorbing nutrients and eliminating waste. Not consuming enough fiber or probiotic-rich foods can lead to digestive problems like bloating, cramping, gas, abdominal pain, and diarrhea. English Tabaie says Americans don't eat nearly enough fiber (the Recommended Dietary Allowance is 25 grams for women, 38 grams for men; most Americans eat about 10 to 15 grams), whereas studies have shown that our ancestors ate up to 100 grams a day. She explains that that alone could be a reason why so many people have GI issues. English Tabaie also stresses the importance of hydration, because if you're increasing fiber intake, more water is needed to move everything through the GI tract.

Smoothies incorporating fiber-rich foods, yogurt, kefir, apples, chia seeds, papaya, beets, ginger, and dark greens can all support digestive issues.

SMOOTHIES TO SUPPORT:
You're Nuts! (p. 145), Super Seed (p.169), Tummy Soother (p. 190)

Immunity

"The ability of the body to stay healthy and fight off disease and infection is closely tied to what we eat," says English Tabaie. "The same factors that link diet to mood disorders—inflammation, oxidative stress, and gut health—also play a role in the health of our immune system. Eating a diet rich in fruits and vegetables has been shown to reduce inflammation and promote healthy immune functioning."

English Tabaie cites studies that have shown that consuming protein from plants, such as pea protein, increases the production of anti-inflammatory molecules in the gut. This is good news for vegetarians, who should also see the next section to make sure they are getting enough protein in their diets.

English Tabaie highlights the importance of both probiotics and prebiotics on metabolic and immune function. Probiotics, live bacteria found in food or supplements, she explains, may beneficially regulate intestinal health and even treat or prevent inflammatory bowel disease. Kefir and yogurt (both dairy-based) are both good sources that can be added to your smoothies and make them creamy and delicious to boot.

Prebiotics, aka food for our microbiome, can be found in pretty much all plants including smoothie-friendly apples, greens, and even grains.

Finally, English Tabaie stresses that both eating too much and eating too little can negatively affect our immune system, which is why it's so important to eat a balanced diet that nourishes the body and prevents cycles of bingeing and restriction.

SMOOTHIES TO SUPPORT:
Golden Milk (p. 182), Immunity Booster (p. 173), Mango Spice (p. 41), Super Greens (p. 72), Apple Beet Ginger (p. 130), Skin Brightener (p. 186)

Candida

Candida is a fungus that aids with nutrient absorption and digestion when it's at proper levels in the body. However, when candida overproduces, it can become a serious health concern. Eliminating yeast and sugary foods from the diet is one of the best ways to reduce and eliminate candida in one's body. Leafy greens, chia seeds, flax, avocado, strawberries, blueberries, blackberries, coconut water, turmeric, ginger, and cinnamon are all beneficial ingredients to add to smoothies.

SMOOTHIES TO SUPPORT:
Tummy Soother (p. 190), Strawberry Coconut (p. 125), Keto-Friendly Double Chocolate (p. 161)

Chemotherapy

Chemotherapy often causes appetite loss and digestion difficulties, making it very hard for patients to get enough calories and nutrients in their bodies. Blending breaks down the fiber in smoothie ingredients, making the food easier for the body to digest. You can pack smoothies with nutrient-dense calories, which makes them a gift in the struggle to keep weight on and one's strength up. It's important to add plenty of fiber-rich foods, ingredients containing potassium, and fluid (for hydration) and to avoid anything spicy. Consult with your doctor about any smoothie regimen you intend to follow.

Getting Protein, B Vitamins, and Other Essential Nutrients into Vegans and Vegetarians

Almost every time I tell someone that my son is a vegetarian, I'm met with questions about how he gets enough protein and other nutrients, such as B vitamins. There's a lot of noise about vegans and vegetarians not having enough sources to choose from, and while omnivores have plenty of options, it's not that much harder for anyone favoring a plant-based diet.

Protein: It's easier than one might think to get the recommended daily amount of protein into your diet entirely via plant-based proteins (USDA guidelines suggest that a person who consumes 2,000 calories a day should be eating around 55 grams of protein, with women needing around 46 grams and men 56 grams). The USDA numbers may sound daunting, but when you start to read the nutritional information on food packaging and then apply it to smoothie making, it all becomes very reassuring. This chart includes some great protein sources for vegetarians and vegans:

FOOD (amount)	AMOUNT OF PROTEIN (in grams)
1% Dairy Milk (1 cup)	8
Soy Milk (1 cup)	7
Pumpkin Seeds (1 tablespoon)	8
Spirulina (1 tablespoon)	4
Spinach (1 cup)	5
Broccoli (1 small, 5-inch stalk)	3.3
Almond Butter (1 tablespoon)	4
Peanut Butter (1 tablespoon)	4
Greek Yogurt (1 cup)	20
Protein Powder (1 scoop)	~ 20
Hemp Seeds (1 tablespoon)	5

B Vitamins: Vegans and vegetarians need to make sure they're getting plenty of B vitamins, which play an important role in maintaining normal physiological and metabolic functions, as well as in energy production and the synthesis and repair of DNA and RNA. They can also promote calmness and maintaining a healthy nervous system and are important in the maintenance of healthy skin and muscle tone. That being said, the body doesn't store B vitamins well, and it is possible to become low in one or more of the B vitamins, which can result in deficiency symptoms like anemia and skin disorders, to name a couple.

Animal-derived foods such as poultry, fish, and eggs are major sources of several of the B vitamins (B12, for instance, is only found in animal products). Luckily, plant sources of B vitamins include whole grains, potatoes, beans, and lentils (none of the recipes in this book feature these foods, but there's no reason you couldn't incorporate them into a smoothie if you so chose), and plenty of my favorite smoothie ingredients include B vitamins: Green leafy vegetables are particularly high in B9 (folate) and there are several types of B vitamins, such as B6, B9, and B12, which can be found in sunflower seeds, almonds, citrus fruits, bananas, and avocados.[5]

5. "Dr. Weil's Guide to B Vitamins," from www.drweil.com.

Super Boosts and Other Key Smoothie Ingredients: A Health Benefits Primer

INGREDIENT	PROPERTIES	BENEFITS
Açaí	This deep purple South American berry is jam-packed with antioxidants, is low in sugar, and contains excellent amounts of calcium, fiber, and vitamin A, as well as being anti-inflammatory. This superfood is available frozen or in freeze-dried powdered form.	Supports heart health and healthy energy levels, enhances skin health, possesses brain-boosting properties.
Almonds	This nut, which is actually a seed encased within the hard-shelled fruit of the almond tree, is full of monounsaturated fatty acids, dietary fiber, and antioxidants. Almonds contain vitamins, including vitamin E and riboflavin, and trace minerals, including calcium and magnesium.	Supports the immune system, regulates metabolism, lowers cholesterol.
Ashwagandha	Another supplement with millennia-old super boost status, this Indian herb is a staple of Ayurvedic medicine. A powdered form made from the leaves or root of the ashwagandha plant, ashwagandha is rich in withanolides, a collection of naturally ocurring steroids, fatty acids, amino acids, and choline.	Ashwagandha is prized for its ability to reduce stress and anxiety. It's also been shown to effectively combat insomnia, improve brain function, boost energy, and lower blood sugar levels. Believed to be a powerful anti-inflammatory and to inhibit tumor growth.
Bee Pollen	The food of the young bee, bee pollen is approximately 40 percent protein (it's a complete protein source) and packed with B vitamins. Bee pollen contains nearly all nutrients required by humans. Enough said.	Aside from being a powerful immunity booster, choosing a locally sourced bee pollen is believed to help reduce seasonal allergies by helping you develop a tolerance for the pollen in your area.
Blue Majik (Blue Algae)	A proprietary extract of the blue-green algae spirulina from the company E3 Live. Much like green spirulina, Blue Majik is nutrient dense and full of vitamins (especially B12), enzymes, and minerals.	Research suggests Blue Majik can support joints, increase energy and endurance, and give antioxidant support. It is also an immunity booster.
Brazil Nuts	Contain the hard-to-find mineral selenium. Just one nut gives you your entire daily dose.	Because selenium is fuel for hormones, specifcially thyroid, it can help calm inflammation and lift moods.
Cacao Powder	Made by cold-pressing unroasted cocoa beans, which maintains its living enzymes and eliminates the fat. This magical antioxidant-packed superfood contains high levels of magnesium flavanoids, calcium, iron, zinc, copper, potassium, and manganese.	Contains significantly more antioxidant compounds than blueberries, goji berries, and pomegranate and is believed to help prevent cancer. A large study revealed higher levels of cacao consumption were associated with lower risk of cardiovascular disease.
Camu Camu	A shrub found in swamps or flooded areas of the Amazon, this superhero contains the most vitamin C of any food source on the planet. Sold as a powder, it's also an incredible source of manganese and carotenoids (antioxidants).	Great for colds and to boost your immunity, camu camu's powerful antioxidants and antiviral ability can also help fight against gum diseases like gingivitis. It also supports bone health.
Cashews	Considered a seed, cashews are high in protein, dietary fiber, essential minerals, and antioxidants and are one of the best sources of copper, iron, and zinc. Lower in fat than most nuts but high in heart-healthy monounsaturated fat.	May reduce risk of cancer and diabetes. Oleic acid promotes heart health; copper helps create enzymes involved in collagen development, supporting skin and hair health; magnesium soothes nerves. Their high levels of filling fiber help manage weight.

INGREDIENT	PROPERTIES	BENEFITS
Chia Seeds	Rich in omega-3 fatty acids, fiber, minerals, and antioxidants, chia seeds are a complete protein source. Two tablespoons have more calcium than a glass of milk. Also high in the minerals magnesium and phosphorus.	These tiny seeds can expand up to nine times in the body, keeping you full longer and aiding in weight loss. Phosphorus and magnesium promote good bone health. Excellent protein source for plant-based diets.
Chlorella	A single-celled green algae, chlorella's exact nutrient content depends on growing conditions, but it's consistently 50 to 65 percent protein (and a complete protein source).	Aside from being full of nutrients, chlorella is alkalizing, a great blood sugar stabilizer, and detoxifying, and it has been known to lower cholesterol.
Cinnamon	An antioxidant powerhouse, cinnamon's secret is sodium benzoate, or NaB, a derivative of the spice known for its antiflammatory, neuroprotective, and neurorestorative properties. Get Ceylon cinnamon, which is a more pure form, whenever possible.	A large study showed a link to a reduced risk of heart disease (a tiny daily serving of just 120 mg lowers levels of total cholesterol). It has also been shown to lower blood sugar levels.
Coconut Oil	High in healthy saturated fats called medium-chain triglycerides (MCTs).	MCTs can reduce hunger, boost fat burning, and provide your body and brain with quick energy. They also raise the good HDL cholesterol in your blood, which is linked to reduced heart disease risk. There are ongoing studies on the potential benefits of coconut oil for Alzheimer's patients.
Collagen Peptides	Collagen is the most abundant protein in the body and a key component of all connective tissues. Collagen peptides contain amino acids, which are identical to the protein found in skin, nails, hair, bones, cartilage, and joints. They dissolve easily, making them a great option for smoothies.	Good for alleviating joint pain and promoting healthy hair, skin, and nails—especially important as we age. May help reduce bone loss. Good source of protein and may contribute to improved metabolic function.
Flax Seeds	One of the oldest cultivated crops, flax is another omega-3 fatty acid source (see DHA above) that comes in the form of alpha-linolenic acid (ALA). Flax is also a good source of B1 (thiamine), magnesium, and copper.	Flax has us covered as a form of fiber and may have other health benefits related to cancer and cardiovascular health. Rich in omega-3s, they're good for your brain and more. Consume flax ground, rather than in whole seed form, to maximize your body's access to its nutrients.
Ginger	This flavorful root with potent wellness properties can be used fresh or powdered. Ginger's primary bioactive compound, gingerol, is a major anti-inflammatory and antioxidant.	Well known for its ability to alleviate nausea, especially during pregnancy. Its anti-imflammatory properties reduce muscle soreness and pain from osteoporosis arthritis. Believed to reduce both cholesterol and blood sugar levels and aid in digestion. Good for boosting immunity.
Goji Berries	A superfood from China with a millennia-old reputation, gojis are brimming with antioxidants and, as a good source of vitamins C and A, iron, zinc, and fiber, they're about as nutrient dense as they come.	Known to increase energy and quality of sleep, boost mental acuity and immunity, and induce calm. Gojis are powerful, so discuss with your doctor if you are taking medication, have issues with blood pressure, or are pregnant or nursing.
Golden Berries	This super berry, which in dried form resembles a deep orange-gold raisin, has a vibrant tropical flavor profile that's both sweet and sour and packs a nutritional punch to boot: golden berries are rich in antioxidants, vitamins, minerals, and fiber. Eating them has been compared to taking a multivitamin.	Powerful anti-inflammatory properties. Golden berries have been used for centuries to help sufferers of asthma and to treat various skin conditions and even optic nerve disorders.

INGREDIENT	PROPERTIES	BENEFITS
Greens Powder/ Supergreens	Generally comprised of a long list of leafy greens, seaweeds, vegetables, grasses, etc., greens powders are smoothie-friendly powders designed to help people get their recommended daily allowance of greens and vegetables. There are all types of greens powders on the market, so nutritional properties will vary.	While consuming fresh (or frozen) vegetables is always preferable, powders are convenient on their own or as a supplement to a well-balanced smoothie. Many powders feature ingredients with benefits like protein or enzymes. Look for brands with high-quality ingredient standards.
Hemp Seeds	High levels (no pun intended) of vitamins A, C, and E, omega-3 fatty acids, and beta-carotene. Packed with magnesium and rich in protein, carbohydrates, minerals, and fiber.	These babies can boost your energy, help keep you feeling full longer, and even help you sleep better. They are an excellent, very digestible protein source—take note, vegetarians and vegans!
Maca	A cruciferous vegetable native to Peru, maca is processed into a powder, either raw or gelatinized (the latter, which I prefer, removes the starch and the nutrients are more concentrated).	Maca is classified as an adaptogen—one of those buzzy herbs believed to help your body fight stress and achieve homeostasis, improving hormone balance and metabolism, and proven to boost stamina and energy.
Maqui Berries	Maqui, mostly found in the US in powdered form, are deep purple berries native to Chile. Maqui possess extremely high levels of powerful antioxidants (anthocyanins and delphinidins). Iron, calcium, and vitamins A and C are also present.	This antioxidant powerhouse has incredible anti-inflammatory properties. Studies point to its ability to lower bad cholesterol and thus the risk of heart disease.
Matcha	This variety of green tea is making a name for itself as a potent source of nutrients and antioxidants, including polyphenols such as the powerful epigallocatechin gallate (EGCG).	Studies show effects ranging from boosting energy and metabolism (and aiding weight loss), to lowering the risk of heart disease, to slowing the growth of cancer cells.
MCT Oil	MCT (medium-chain triglyceride) oil is most commonly extracted from coconut oil (more than 50% of the fat in coconut oil comes from MCTs).	Antibacterial and antiviral properties may help balance gut flora and support immune health. Is easy to digest (making it a good source of fat for those who cannot tolerate other types of fats) and helps suppress hunger.
Nut Butter	A paste obtained by grinding almost any type of nut. Opt for organic versions (especially peanut butter) featuring one ingredient only—nuts!	There are almost as many types of nut butters as there are nuts, so I won't go into all of them here. However, the health benefits for almonds, cashews, and walnuts are all listed elsewhere on this chart and obviously apply here as well.
Pumpkin Seeds/ Pepitas	Also known as pumpkin seeds, pepitas are nutrient packed. Rich in antioxidants, magnesium, and phosphorus, they're also a good source of protein, iron, and zinc.	Studies support pepitas contribution to good heart health, fertility, and improved sleep, mood, and energy. They also may reduce inflammation and help prevent some types of cancer.
Pink Himalayan Salt	Know as the cleanest salt available, it contains more than eighty-four minerals and trace elements, including calcium, magnesium, potassium, copper, and iron, making it a healthier option than table salt.	While I like using this type of salt in my smoothies, I wouldn't depend on it as a source of any of its minerals; however, salt can help with the absorption of nutrients.

INGREDIENT	PROPERTIES	BENEFITS
Probiotic Powder	Gut-friendly bacteria in convenient powders or capsules that can be opened up and added to smoothies.	Maintaining a healthy gut is essential not only to digestion, but overall physical and mental well-being. Probiotics help your gut perform its best and promote a healthy balance of bacteria in the body. It's important to note that strain and quality matter when it comes to choosing your probiotic.
Reishi	A fungi with deep roots in Eastern medicine, reishi mushroom can commonly be found in smoothie-friendly powdered form.	Reishi have been shown to have powerful immunity-boosting properties and have neuroprotective properities that can help support memory and improve mood.
Seed Butters	Much like their nutty friends, seed butters are produced by grinding seeds into paste. The most widely available are sunflower, pumpkin seed, flax, hemp, and seed butter combos made from a variety of seeds.	A great option for those with tree nut allergies, most are nutrient rich and many are lower in calories than nut butters. They contain the same health benefits as the seeds they are made from.
Spirulina	One of the most nutrient-dense foods on the planet, spirulina is packed with vitamins B1, 2, and 3, iron (more than spinach!), magnesium, iron, and potassium. Low in calories; high in protein and chlorophyll (thus its deep green color); powerful antioxidant and anti-inflammatory properties.	Spirulina is a nutrient bomb and an immunity booster. Known for its incredible detoxingfying capabilities, spirulina also supports endurance and muscle strength and can lower the risk of heart disease. Good protein source for vegans and vegetarians.
Turmeric	This culinary spice has powerful antioxidant and anti-inflammatory properties. You can use the whole root or the powdered form. To obtain the full benefits of its most powerful compound, curcumin, combine turmeric with black pepper and a fat, as our bodies have difficulty absorbing it on its own.	Wonderful for everything from arthritis to boosting immunity to supporting healthy joints to brain health.
Vanilla Bean	The fruits of a few very particular kinds of orchids. Because of their rarity, whole vanilla beans are likely the most expensive spice in our cupboards. It's on the list more for its wonderful flavor than its nutritional value.	Good for your nose and taste buds! You can get vanilla in whole bean form or in a paste or extract.
Walnuts	Contain a powerful combination of antioxidants not found in many other foods. Higher in omega-3s than any other nut, they're also loaded with fiber, minerals, essential vitamins and fats, and vitamin E. One-quarter cup of walnuts provides more than 100 percent of the daily recommended value of omega-3 fats, along with high amounts of copper, manganese, and biotin.	Combating inflammation, improving brain performance, and reducing risk of heart disease are just some of the health benefits suggested by studies on walnuts. They're a great source of omega-3 fats for vegetarians and vegans.

Maximum Vitamin Absorption

While flavor is essential, we primarily drink smoothies for nutrients, vitamins, and minerals, so it makes sense that we should consider how to optimize their nutritional potential. I remember when I first learned about turmeric (a root in the ginger family) and its robust anti-inflammatory properties. I started using it in my cooking, believing I was reaping all the benefits it had to offer, when months later, a friend told me that without combining it with other specific ingredients, it wasn't being absorbed properly in my body. I was happy to learn that fact, but also frustrated that I was under the impression I was making a major contribution to my diet when in fact I wasn't. It made me consider how many other powerful ingredients I might be failing to get the most out of.

I'm grateful to be able to have regular conversations with incredible doctors, nutritionists, and health practitioners like Ashley Koff, RD, CEO of the Better Nutrition Program and author of several books. Recently, Ashley and I were discussing the importance of not only eating nutritious foods, but also being aware of how eating certain foods together can increase our ability to absorb the vitamins and minerals in those foods.

"Nutrients are not islands," says Ashley. "They work in concert with other nutrients to give your body what it needs to run better. Some nutrients actually help others get where they need to go, so it's critical you get these escort nutrients at the same time you get in the others for optimal effect." For example, consuming turmeric with a fat like nuts or coconut oil and a crack of black pepper is essential if we want to derive that powerful root's full potential benefits. Here are a few more nutrients that will help others when it comes to absorption.

Vitamin D (found in dairy-rich foods, fortified orange juice, and soy milk) helps calcium absorption.

Vitamin C (found in kale, kiwi, broccoli, lemon, papaya, strawberry, and orange) aids with iron absorption.

Healthy fats like the ones found in avocado, nuts, chia seeds, and coconut help antioxidants and vitamins like A, D, E, and K to be absorbed for use.

Ashley adds that "Liquid nutrition (like drinking smoothies) is another way to help your body absorb nutrients, especially when your body is stressed or trying to heal. When food is in the form of a liquid, your body has less work to do digestively, so nutrients can get where they need to go easier and faster."

The recipes in this book were developed to pair complementary ingredients to enhance nutrient absorption so you are sure to get the most out of your smoothies.

SMOOTHIE HACK

Shopping Smart: 1. Find your local store with the best prices: Trader Joe's, Costco, Aldi, and even Walmart all have competitively priced organic fresh and frozen produce, milks, nuts, seeds, and powders all year long. 2. Ask for seconds: Vendors at your local farmers' market may have "seconds," which is how farmers refer to their overripe, bruised, or blemished produce. Also, bananas are the base for so many smoothie recipes, so look for overly ripe bananas at the grocery store. In this state they are perfect to slice and freeze for future smoothie making. You can often purchase overripe or blemished produce at a steep discount.

Fresh or Frozen?

When it comes to picking fresh or frozen ingredients to add to your smoothies, there are several basic factors to consider: seasonality, temperature preference, and cost.

For the recipes in this book, I specify whether to use fresh or frozen ingredients if I have a personal preference, but you should feel free to adapt the recipes based on the temperatures and textures you prefer and what you have on hand. When it doesn't make much of a difference, I will let you know when you can use fresh or frozen ingredients interchangeably.

FRESH

I've been going to my local farmers' market every week for almost two decades and always have a counter and fridge full of fresh produce that I use for my smoothies. When you buy fresh fruit and veg in season, especially if it's from a local farm you love, you can usually be assured it's been picked very recently. Fresh fruit is also great for freezing to have off season.

I almost always use fresh produce when it comes to my greens, carrots, and other vegetables in my smoothies, and I tend to choose frozen more often when it comes to fruit. I prefer some balance when it comes to temperature and texture. For example, people who don't like a thicker, colder smoothie may opt to use fresh strawberries when they're in season instead of frozen (or vice versa).

FROZEN

I keep my freezer stocked with a variety of organic frozen fruits and vegetables so I can make smoothies whenever I want. Ounce for ounce, frozen produce often costs less than fresh, making it budget friendly. Frozen produce is picked and flash-frozen at the peak of perfection, so it can have even more nutrients than fresh produce, which can sit on grocery store shelves for days or weeks at a time, losing valuable nutrients. Also, I'm a stickler for not wasting food, so I love how frozen produce allows you to use the exact amount you need with no spoilage.

Here's a list of what I keep on hand at all times to make living the Smoothie Project convenient and affordable. This may seem like a lot of frozen produce, but remember, it will stay fresh for months and make your life considerably easier, especially if you've got multiple smoothie drinkers living under your roof, or if like me you want to try a different smoothie recipe every day. Variety allows you to be more creative and makes smoothie prep a lot easier.

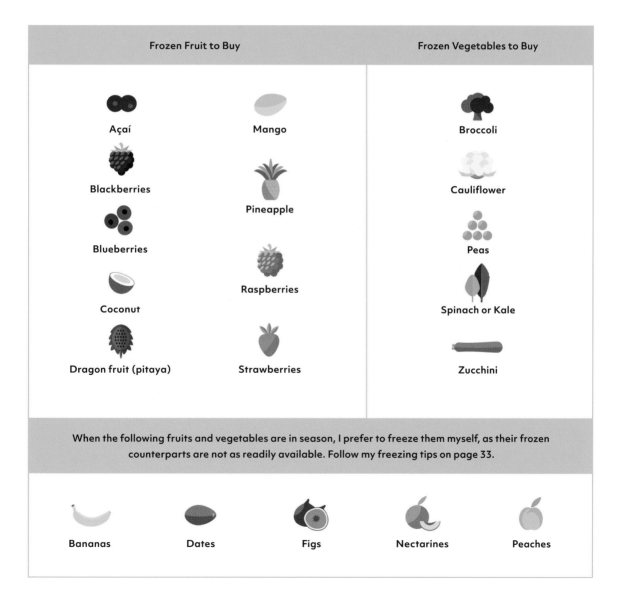

Frozen Fruit to Buy		Frozen Vegetables to Buy
Açaí	Mango	Broccoli
Blackberries	Pineapple	Cauliflower
Blueberries	Raspberries	Peas
Coconut		Spinach or Kale
Dragon fruit (pitaya)	Strawberries	Zucchini

When the following fruits and vegetables are in season, I prefer to freeze them myself, as their frozen counterparts are not as readily available. Follow my freezing tips on page 33.

| Bananas | Dates | Figs | Nectarines | Peaches |

Choosing Your Liquid

To make a smoothie, you need to blend your fruits, vegetables, or other solid ingredients with a liquid. Many of the recipes in this book are flexible, giving you the option of using any milk that you prefer, whether it be cow's milk or a plant-based milk. Others recommend a particular milk or other liquid, such as water or tea, if I think that the flavor of the recipe benefits from a specific choice. However, you should always choose the liquid that is right for you—and you have a lot of options at your disposal.

Most of us grew up with one kind of milk—the kind from a cow (choice in those days was limited to whole, skim, and 2%). These days options abound: cow's milk, nut milks, soy milk, rice milk, oat milk, hemp milk, kefir. . . . The list seems endless, and knowing which one to choose can be overwhelming, not just from a flavor profile standpoint, but also because the nutritional profiles vary. See the chart on page 248 to help you select your liquid, taking concerns like calories, dairy vs. plant-based, and health issues into account. It is also important to consider the following:

Flavor: The flavor profile of the milk you use plays a large role in determining how your smoothie turns out, so have a bit of fun discovering what kind you prefer. It's worth sampling as much as you can. You may just find a milk for life.

Brand: For years my husband thought he hated rice milk until he tried some from a different brand and found the taste to be completely unlike what he had associated with rice milk. Many variables can affect the taste and texture of the same kind of milk, from the type and quality of the nut or grain being used to produce the milk to how the milk is processed (for example, one brand's almond milk can be much thicker and creamier than another's), so be open to trying different brands. In turn, every brand can produce a slightly different result in a smoothie. I also find that shelf-stable milks can taste different than their refrigerated counterparts. What's more, some companies use additives, which affect everything from the flavor of the milk to its shelf life, so in addition to tasting around, it's a good idea to read labels to see what you're ingesting. Finally, it's important to mention that when buying almond and other plant-based milks, avoid brands containing carrageenan, a food additive used to thicken milk which studies have linked to inflammation as well as certain types of cancers.

In a DIY mood?

You can make your own nut milks if you like. Most are fairly simple processes, and recipes are easy to find on the internet. I occasionally make my own almond milk with whole almonds (page 249). I find it to be more delicious than any brand I've ever bought in the store. It's super easy to make, but the almonds do need to be soaked beforehand, so it's not a quickie recipe. But if you find yourself in a pinch, blend 1 cup (240 ml) of water per 1 tablespoon almond butter, a sprinkle of salt, and a touch of maple syrup. You'll be surprised at how yummy this shortcut almond milk is.

Worry not. Coconut water, herbal teas, and even water can be used in place of milks in your smoothies, the latter two also being far less expensive options. Herbal teas are great because they have zero calories and there are infinite flavor options to experiment with.

Finding a liquid you love is worth the effort of some experimentation. Ask around to see what your friends like, be open to trying new types, and see what tastes best and works with your dietary needs and goals.

Want to lighten the calorie count of your smoothie? Use water, herbal tea, or one of the lower calorie milks (see the chart on page 248) as your liquid. The fruit, vegetables, and other ingredients will still provide tons of flavor. Also, using water is another way to save money.

Got Milks? Breaking Down the Differences

You may want to rely solely on your taste buds or dietary needs to choose your liquid, but here's a breakdown/cheat sheet to see how nine different types of milks[6] (and one liquid) compare on paper.

MILK TYPE	PROS	CONS
Almond Milk	Low in sodium; carb and sugar free; highest calcium source of all milk options, even cow's	Contrary to what you might think, not high in protein, especially compared to other milk options
Cow's Milk	Choose from skim, 1%, and 2%; high in protein (and a complete protein), calcium, and B12; most nutritious of all the options	Higher in saturated fat than plant-based milks
Oat Milk	High in soluble fiber; contains beta-glucans and more B vitamins than soy or coconut milk; good alternative for people with nut and soy allergies	Low in protein, vitamins, and minerals; contains more fat than other milk options
Hemp Milk	Creamy; rich in omega-3 fatty acids that can help keep cholesterol levels and blood pressure in check	Has more fat than other milk options
Kefir *a fermented milk made from cow, goat, or sheep milk; tastes similar to yogurt*	High in beneficial yeast, probiotic bacteria, protein, calcium, and vitamins D and B12	May cause constipation and/or intestinal cramping
Rice Milk	The most hypoallergenic of all the milk options, it's also the sweetest; very low in fat; and contains high levels of magnesium	Low in calcium and protein; significantly higher in carbs, calories, and sugars than the other options
Soy Milk	Highest in protein of the plant-based milks except pea and is a complete protein; low in sodium	The soy estrogens in soy milk can affect hormonal balance; one of the highest in fat and lowest in calcium of the alternative milks
Pea Milk	Vegan, nut, soy, lactose, and gluten free, it's better for the environment than almond and cow milk and has more protein and calcium than other alternative milks*	Not many beyond saying "pea milk." It doesn't even taste like peas.
Coconut Milk	Low in calories, creamy texture similar to cow's milk, very flavorful	No protein; high in saturated fat, but some nutritionists argue that these are medium-chain fatty acids, which only raise good cholesterol
Coconut Water *not milk, but who's counting?*	High in potassium; low in calories; hydrating; not processed	High in sodium

6. *"The Differences Between 8 Kinds of Milk," Mother Nature Network, 1.31.18*

Homemade Nut Milk

Makes 4½ cups (1 liter)

Ingredients:

4 cups (940 ml) filtered water, plus extra for soaking

1 cup (140 g) raw almonds (or your favorite nut)

2 tablespoons agave nectar or honey

¼ teaspoon vanilla extract or ⅛ teaspoon vanilla paste

Place the almonds in a large bowl and cover with water. Cover with a dish towel. Soak for at least 4 hours, or up to overnight on the counter.

Drain the almonds and place them in a blender with the agave, vanilla, and 4 cups (940 ml) water. Blend until the almonds are in tiny pieces.*

Place a strainer in a large bowl and cover the top of the strainer with several layers of cheesecloth, a nut milk bag, or a clean tea towel (this step is important because the almond pieces will be so small that the cheesecloth is needed to stop them from going into the milk).

Pour the almond milk through the cheesecloth. You may need to do this in stages so the milk can slowly strain through. Use a spoon to scrape the bottom of the cheesecloth so all of the milk can pass through.

Pour the milk into a container, cover, and refrigerate until ready to drink, for up to 5 days.

*The blended almonds can be stored in an airtight container in the refrigerator for up to a week to be added to smoothies, eaten as a breakfast cereal with standard oatmeal toppings, as a dessert topped with fresh berries, or even added to cookies to give them an extra protein boost.

There are some great nut milks you can buy at the grocery, but there are fresh homemade nut milks that will truly change your world and taste buds forever. I started making this almond milk when my son was just over a year old. I would fill his little cup with a few ounces and watch him guzzle it down.

Making homemade nut milk is easy but requires a bit of time to soak the nuts, so make sure to factor that into your plans. For smoothie purists, it's the icing on the cake. Don't take my word for it, though. Try making this recipe just once—I promise you'll agree it's worth the effort.

Replace the almonds with the same amount of cashews, walnuts, Brazil nuts, pecans, or macadamia nuts, if you prefer a different kind of nut milk.

Nuts: To Soak or Not to Soak

While not essential, soaking raw nuts overnight in water can be beneficial. Soaking nuts enhances them from a nutritional standpoint, enabling your body to absorb more of their vitamins and minerals. Soaking nuts also reduces the enzyme inhibitors present in the nut, helping to make digestion efficient. What's more, the nuts become softer and easier to digest, and are almost velvety when blended, making for a creamier smoothie. You can also buy sprouted versions of many nuts, which interact with your body the same way soaked ones do.

Second, consider the strength of your blender. How well does it puree harder varieties like walnuts, almonds, and Brazil nuts? If you don't have the strongest of motors and often find bits of nuts in your smoothie, soaking them first will soften them and make pureeing a breeze.

Soaking nuts is also an essential part of making your own nut milks, which I find extremely satisfying. If you're interested in doing this, I have a recipe for homemade almond milk on the previous page. It's a recipe that can be applied to most nuts, but if there's a particular nut you want to make a milk from and are unsure, search around online to find a recipe you like.

Soaking nuts is easy: Place them in a bowl, cover with water, and soak for at least 1 hour, but preferably overnight. Drain off any liquid and add the nuts to your blender with the rest of your smoothie's ingredients. The remainder of the soaked nuts can be refrigerated for a week, so if you're making smoothies every day, you can soak a big batch to make life easier.

Acknowledgments

The idea for this book began with a mother wanting to help her son. It evolved into something bigger—a healing lifestyle shift for the #smoothieproject community that accompanied me on this journey. I'm deeply grateful to you for your support, as well as to the Weelicious followers who I've been blessed to connect with daily for well over a decade.

My thanks go out to:

Kenya, TSP's first subject and my culinary muse.

Chloe, who taught me to open my eyes to foods that I'd closed the door on.

Gemma, who's brought our family endless joy from the moment she arrived and will forever be known as our smoothie baby.

Alison Fargis—we connected immediately and I'm so grateful that you led me to Abrams.

Laura Dozier, whose sharp instincts and invaluable direction helped make this book the best it could be. To the entire Abrams team, including Deb, Jennifer, Connor, and Hayley, thank you for helping me create the book of my dreams.

Colin—you're a true genius. Your keen eye and light transformed the most simple ingredients into pure magic.

Heidi Robb, what would I have done without you?

Keri, Ashley, Whitney, Kelly, Katie, Heng, Natasha, Sydney, and Aida, my nutritional/eco/holistic dream team. I've benefited endlessly from your knowledge and experience.

Alex, Dana, Gaby, Juliet, Maya, and Staci, my dear friends and sounding boards, who've been there with me on this project every step of the way.

Melissa—what did I ever do to deserve you?

Jackson and Otis, for being sweet enough to come drink (and drink) smoothies.

Cheryl, you really know how to clean a girl up. Your talent, heart, and kindness know no bounds.

Sunshine Sachs (Keleigh, Megan, Lauren, and Sandra), the ninjas who've helped get TSP in front of more eyeballs than I ever imagined.

Melissa's Produce and Robert, for the gorgeous fresh produce that graces the pages of this book.

Jenine and Eliana, who make better decisions for me than I could make for myself.

Charles, Sarah Anne, April, and Danielle, thank you for making our shoot such a gratifying, fun experience.

Andi, who helped me stay on top of everything.

The incredible brands like Philips, Kitchen Aid, Breville, Vitamix, Siggi's, Stonyfield, Ora Organics, PlantFusion, Artisana, Wild Friends, Orgain, Navitas, Sunfood, Amazing Grass, Garden of Life, Vital Proteins, Bulletproof, Primal Kitchen, Ancient Nutrition, Sunwarrior, Nutiva, Justin's, Terrasoul, Aloha Protein, Pitaya Plus, Forager Project, E3Live, Green Vibrance, Malk, New Barn, Califia, Wallaby, and Ripple Foods who donated their products for recipe testing and photography.

Mom, Dad, Viv, Sonny, and Judi for being the best examples of parents, grandparents, and friends.

Lastly, to Jon. Tireless, passionate, and, most of all, the best husband and father. This book wouldn't exist without your unwavering support. I look forward to the day we get to sail into the sunset, smoothies in hand, of course.

Index

Editor: Laura Dozier
Designer: TPD Design House
Production Manager: Kathleen Gaffney

Library of Congress Control Number: 2019930864

ISBN: 978-1-4197-4042-8
eISBN: 978-1-68335-753-7

Printed and bound in the United States
10 9 8 7 6 5 4 3 2

Abrams books are available at special discounts when
purchased in quantity for premiums and promotions
as well as fundraising or educational use. Special
editions can also be created to specification. For
details, contact specialsales@abramsbooks.com or the
address below.

Abrams® is a registered trademark of
Harry N. Abrams, Inc.

ABRAMS The Art of Books
195 Broadway, New York, NY 10007
abramsbooks.com